AUTOGEDDON

AUTOGEDDON

Heathcote Williams

JONATHAN CAPE
LONDON

Contents

A carriage without horse shall go
Disaster fill the world with woe.

From The Prophecies of Mother Shipton,
Ursula Southall of Knaresborough,
Yorkshire, 1488 to 1561

What good is speed if the brain has oozed
out on the way?

Karl Kraus

Today I must resolve to come home in a new
Mustang, Mustang, Mustang.

Sirhan Sirhan (Robert Kennedy's assassin),
Notebooks, May 18th, 1968

In 1885 Karl Benz constructed the first automobile.
It had three wheels, like an invalid car,

And ran on alcohol, like many drivers.

Since then more than seventeen million people have been
    killed
In an undeclared war.

And the rest of the world may be in danger of being run over
In a terminal squabble over their oil.

Were an Alien Visitor
To hover a few hundred yards above the planet
It could be forgiven for thinking
That cars were the dominant life-form,
And that human beings were a kind of ambulatory fuel cell,
Injected when the car wished to move off,
And ejected when they were spent.

If the Visitor's curiosity were still aroused
It would quickly discover on landing,
From hoardings, newspapers and television commercials,
That the car appeared to satisfy a compendious spectrum of
    desires:
Sexual,

Social,

Economic

And religious,

Gratifying an A to Z of unbridled cravings
In the guise of getting from A to B.

Nothing performs like a Saab.
Car as stud.

Beautiful body. A joy to handle. And rumoured to be rather fast –
  MG.
Car as pimp.

Step on the Exhilarator – Datsun.
Car as marital aid.

Drive it like you hate it – Volvo.
Car as enemy. The enemy only you can control.

Believe in Freedom. Believe in Honda.
Car as Universal Declaration of Human Rights,
Drafted with you alone in mind.

Nothing quite so perfectly reflects one's achievements in life –
  Daimler.
A car that gives you permanent positive feedback
And insulates you from any other.

For people who lead the good life.
A car that leads the simple life – Honda.
How to radiate a high-minded Vegan glow
While eating steak tartare.

Crunchy on the outside and hard in the middle – VW Polo.
Car as confectionery.

Kiss the old ideas goodbye – BMW.
Car as mind-stylist.

The Ecstasy without the Agony – Porsche.
The designer drug with no earthly withdrawal symptoms.

The TR7 is now available with optional breezes, sunsets, moon,
Stars, and smell of morning dew.
Car as Nobel Prize for Literature.

Volvo. A car with standards.
For those who might not have any.

Solara – The Power to Light up your Life.
The Holy Grail on wheels.

Rover offers to put you in the Seat of Power
And your passengers in Positions of Privilege.
Car as one-man coup d'état.

Experience more breathing space – Mercedes.
Car as lebensraum.
With 80 per cent of air pollution coming from cars
The additional breathing space may be no wider
Than the walls of a coffin.

Makers of accessories and spare parts,
Known in the trade as 'the fluff',
Are not to be outdone in their inflated claims:
A monstrous close-up of a tyre-tread
Is captioned *The Basic Pattern of Life* –
Fathom the fundamental mysteries of evolution.
Bring primaeval chaos bang up to date.
A competitor peddles *The Tyre that Saves Petrol*;
In the further interest of economy
This rubber time-bomb, like all its counterparts,
May unpredictably explode.

The Visitor moves in for a closer look:
Vehicles are being washed,
Caressed, polished and petted
As if they were members of the family.

A scratch on the body-work
Draws a fury otherwise reserved for child-molesters.

Techno-tomcats appear to spray the boundaries of their
 territory

Marking out the vehicles
With a myriad of autovotive fetishes;

Bumper-stickers
And monogrammic numbers
Are applied as if summoning the menacing potencies
Of the Golem,
A monster lurching through the back-streets,
Its power derived from the cabbalistic marks
Etched upon its forehead;
Pendulous mascots,
Cosy spells against the evils of chance,
Hang like household gods in a home from home.

The inhabitants of North America
Spend sixty-two thousand years a week
Inside these prosthetic tin-cans
Interminably punched out in cybernetic grease-pits
Under militaristic conditions.

Perplexed by the frequency
With which these containers are gouged open
And spattered with the blood of their contents,
The Visitor seeks a pattern
In an echoing Black Museum of soundbites:

'Drivin' along in my automobile,
No particular place to go,
Cruisin' an' playing the radio . . .'

    CRASH

'For Christ's sake, get that child to stop whining . . .'

    CRASH

'I can do this bit of the journey in my sleep . . .'

CRASH

'Uh, there's a fly in my eye . . .'

CRASH

'Look, girl,
Telling someone he's a bad driver
Is like telling him he's a bad fuck.'

'So . . . ?'

CRASH

'Whaddya mean, I'm drunk?
'Course I'm bloody drunk.
The only time I can bloody concentrate's
When I'm bloody drunk . . .'

CRASH

'Ronnie . . .'
'Now what?'
'I'm going to have a baby . . .'

CRASH

'We're on holiday,
So shut up and start enjoying yourselves.'

CRASH

'I wish I was dead.'

CRASH

'You ever feel something's gonna happen and then it does?'
'Nope . . .'

    CRASH

On entry, the automobile –
Even that moving Parthenon, the Rolls –
Agitates the heartbeat
And transforms the psycho-galvanic skin response
Sufficiently to set the needles shivering
On any lie-detector.

From the moment the driver
Settles behind the wheel
Stress readings increase,
As the driver's body is slowly marinated with adreno-toxins
Generating a wide range of cardio-vascular pressures.
The pelvis is fondled by replica flesh oozing with static,
And the automobile becomes an orgone-accumulator
Stimulating shallow sexuality.

Tides of blood and water within the body
Are magi-mixed, as if subject to a permanent full moon.
The car whips up a portable mistral
Of enervating ions

And moves them along in a packet of pre-storm tension:
'Oh we had such an awful journey,
I feel completely washed out . . .
What are we doing here anyway?'

Insulated from the outside world
By the wraparound TV of the car,
The driver's brainwaves are sucked into an artificial
   resonance,
Rendering the dangers as unreal
As those in a video game.

The machine vamps up the muscle power of the driver
With scant relation to the pressure on the pedal:
Half-a-ton is despatched with a feather-like touch.
'Whoops, did we hit something then?'
'Couldn't have. We'd have felt it.'

The vibratory hum of each driver's engine
Swells an onslaught of erosive sound-porn,
Deadening the psyche,

As rush-hour drivers mass together
In a compulsive and pleasureless spectacle
Of mechanical self-abuse.

Civilisation's distinguishing call
Resembles a harsh bottom A,
A penetrative drawling of ninety decibels.
Rats exposed to such levels
Exhibit overt aggression
And no longer nurture their young.

The infra-sound
Exuded by compressors in air-conditioned models
Will deal with those who shrug and claim to be unaffected,
As their pre-capillaries pop
And turn into varicose veins.

Cavernous sides of buildings amplify the volume
As colliding blasts of noise judder back and forth.
Birdsong is sucked down and asphyxiated
Beneath a characterless swamp of sound.

More disturbed citizens seem mesmerised
By traffic's death-rattle.
They stand around devitalised, harassed,
Making incoherent gestures
As if exhausted by vain attempts
To refuse their auditory diet,
Their metabolism jammed by the hormone
Summoned to deal with stressful sound.
Corticotrophin.
A substance that dulls the acoustic nerve,
Rendering any still, small voice
Quite speechless.

Noise becomes an autocratic force
Requiring impotent consent.

The attention span is whittled down
To the length of a passing car:
Look out of any city window –
Cars will slice through your thoughts
And take them away for nothing.

No child knows silence.

Stand on any street
Awash with bristling piranhas
Grinding out the flatulent muzak of stress.
A sudden move, a moment's inattention:
You're snapped up
And idly spat aside.

As adults are glutted by mobility,
Children wanting to play on their own doorsteps
Are hemmed in by parental fears,
Or else fatally immobilised.

The heart of the community, the street,
Is daily rent apart –

Conversation numbed
By a nervy descant of toxic shock.
Streets, once the open forum of daily life,
Are now the open sewers of the car cult.

Its invitations to enlist
Are riddled with a dizzying mumbo-jumbo:
'STEP INTO A WORLD OF ADVANCED ENGINEERING
THROTTLE-BODY ELECTRONIC FUEL INJECTION,
SMOOTH-SKIN BODY SHELL,
FIN-DRUM BRAKES WITH POWER-ASSIST, MEMORY-RETURN
    SEAT-ADJUSTER,
STEEL-BELTED RADIALS, TACHOMETER AND FULL-WIDTH FRONT
    SPOILER,
POWER-OPERATED MOON-ROOF, NEGATIVE ROLL RADIUS,
TELE-TOUCH FOR AUTOMATIC TRANSMISSION,
AND IT SPEAKS THROUGH THE STEERING IN POSITIVE,
    REASSURING TONES . . .
OOOH THE FEEL OF IT – IT TRACKS STRAIGHT AS A LASER
. . . COME AND HAVE ALL THE MUSCLE YOU CAN HANDLE
WITHOUT NEEDING A WHOLE LOT OF MUSCLE TO HANDLE IT.'

Should the torments of this secular mass movement
Drive you steadily round the bend,
Feel free to take it out on anyone you wish,
Including yourself,
With a relaxing impunity.

The Visitor follows up the court reports:
Hit someone over the head with a discarded chrome fender
And kill them:
Life.

Take the precaution of attaching the fender to a car
And kill them:
Six months,
Licence to drive briefly suspended.

The sight of dead animals being disassembled,
Chopped up and ground into meat
On a Chicago packing plant's moving belt
Gave Henry Ford the billion-dollar notion
Of the mass assembly line.

The Nazi autobahns, built with slave labour,
For the conquest of Europe
Were partly funded by Henry Ford.

The Führer kept a signed photograph of Ford
On his desk in the Reich Chancellory,
And in August 1938 awarded him the Grand Cross of the
    German Eagle,
A decoration for distinguished and helpful foreigners.

'I'm going to democratise the automobile,' said Ford,
'And when I'm through everyone will be able to afford one
And about everyone will have one . . .'

Now, we've reached halfway house:
Half the world's earnings are auto-related,
Half the world's resources are auto-devoted
And half the world will be involved in an auto-accident
At some time during their lives.

What Ford and Hitler started
The motor corporations
Appear to be completing,
Offering the ingenious defence
That 'accidents will happen'.

Carbon monoxide,
Since its victims offered least resistance,
Was the death-camp gas that first found Hitler's favour.
Now massive dosages of carbon monoxide
Are apathetically inhaled
Throughout a global Autoreich.

The new theatre of war
Presents itself as a place of leisured entertainment
But, like some benighted South American stadium,
It conceals an unpublicised death-zone . . .

Seventeen million dead,
And counting.

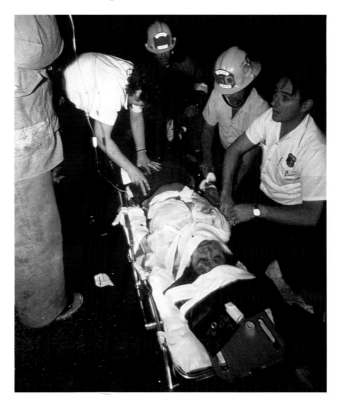

More than twice the number in the death-camps.

Eighteen times the count in Korea.

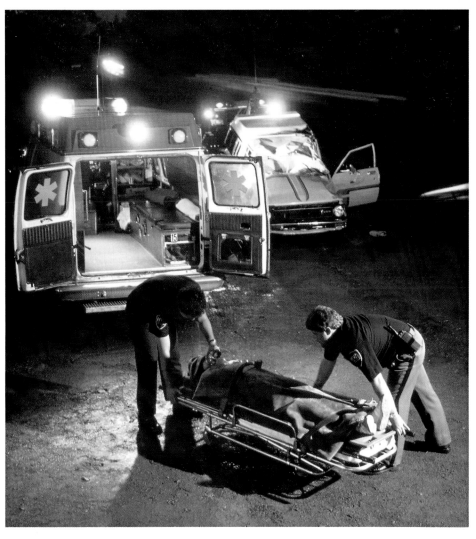

Seventeen Vietnams.

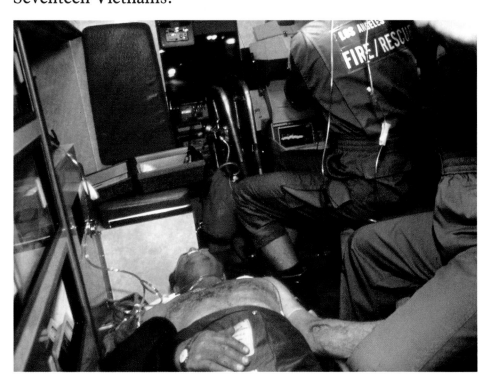

A hundred and thirty times the kill at Hiroshima.

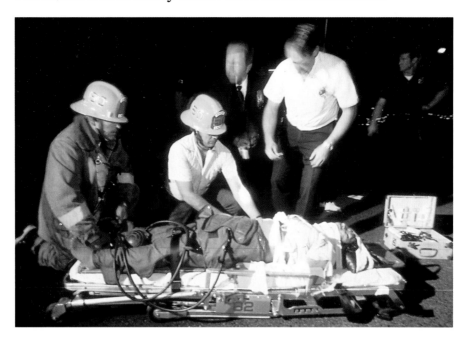

Eight thousand five hundred Ulsters . . .

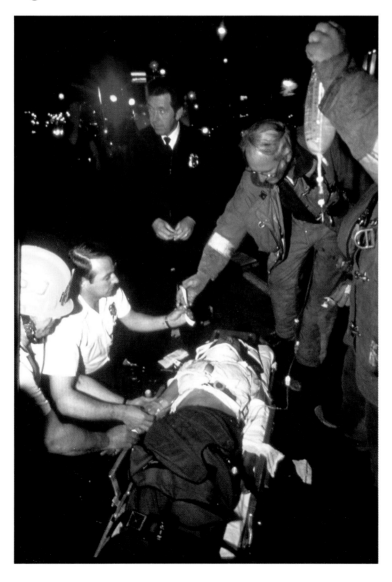

The Hundred Years war in a week.
The Crusades in under thirty seconds.
A humdrum holocaust:
The Third World War nobody bothered to declare.

The victims are brought in on stiff-scoops
To body-workers and brain-repairers
In medical parking lots.

Lines of metal beds on castors:
The unreported wounded, the unreported dying
From the consumer front,
Vainly trying to kick their engines over
And get back on the road.

Sinuous tangles of drip-feeds
Fuel those who blended too urgently with vehicles
And make the room almost indistinguishable
From an automobile's wiring system.

An attendant mops up blood-slick in the corridors
Twenty-four hours a day
Watched by its donors
As they desperately try to steer their minds
Back to a mental oasis
Where the accident never happened.

A child,
Its eyes fried into deep, dried-up hollows,
Stares from within at an unending film-loop
Of a friendly and faithful Ford Cortina
Running amok in a pedestrian precinct
And then exploding.

A girl
With the incised and swollen face of a gargoyle,
Slowly cranks her head down to study the rest of her body:
The inside of her right thigh is torn and braised
By a head-lamp socket;
Her stomach diagonally imprinted and crushed
By *The Basic Pattern of Life*.

A man, badly burned,
Covered with pinched packages of skin

Like a crocodile,
Tries to get up,
Then falls back in agitation,
Wondering why the comforting juices in his brain,
Normally on tap for a reassuring rush,
Are all dried up.
Fretfully, he knocks his forehead
Against the bars of his truckle bed,
As if to stir them back to life.

In the next bed
A woman explains what happened to her
In a voice flattened by repetition:
'I was propelled into it
As if it wasn't happening.
I remember thinking, "Oh, this is that dream you were
    having."
The car crumpled round me.
The windscreen turned into thousands of diamonds.
I screamed and screamed,
Like they do on television.
People came to look through the window
But they went away.
Then someone leant in and handed me a drink,
And said: "I don't know how you survived."'

She turns, unsettled,
And adds a questioning thought,
Repressed till now:
'You can get cancer after an accident, can't you?
Because of the shock.
You don't think I will?'
Dimly aware that when a body is confused,
Like hers,
Cells can attack themselves.

A year later
Her inner organs alive with irradiated pain,
Her head shaven and bloated by chemotherapy,
She dies.

One man sees only glaring headlights,
Fused to his mind's eye
As if by a soldering iron,
All other lucidity extinguished by trauma.
He is permanently silent,
Choosing catatonia as the only protection left.

Another sucks at a hospital sheet in slow motion,
Cosseting the last fraction of life.

A baby held in its mother's arms,
Flung at the dashboard at thirty miles an hour
With the impact of a quarter of a ton,
Is flattened.

In the operating theatre
Many of these wrecks, yesterday's models,
Are decommissioned by assembly-line surgeons,
Their brains idle,
Their throttle closed . . .
Disposable mini-martyrs
To Progress's seedy pretender: traffic.

Surviving victims
Stare out through heretical scars,
Medievally resented and ostracised –
Unlike their inanimate assailants.

The police return home:
'. . . the ketchup came out of the bottle tonight.'
'Yes.'
'You couldn't do fatals unless you have a bit of a laugh.'
'No' – followed by embarrassed remorse –
'Kids are bad though. Ones with kids.'
'Yeah.'

The self is inflated,
Then deflated,
In a lemming rhythm of auto-destruction.
Half a million auto-fatalities per annum.
The fast-food-junk-death-road-show.

'Oh, he died in a car crash . . .'
'She died in a smash-up . . .'
So frequently said
With little more than a careless shrug.
So many swindled of a more measured death.
Accidents feature on the radio
Merely as hold-ups to the traffic flow.

Those that are left behind
Deny it has happened . . .
Laying a place for dinner,
Night after night,
Month after month.

With their haunted cemetery air,
Bathed in ghoulish sodium light,
The motorways seem thick
With demented souls
Suddenly sucked out of twisted metal;
Their bodies randomly pulped by strangers,
Smeared into concrete, trapped in tarmac,
And snarled up with angry disbelief,
Still resonating 'Why ME?
Why ME?'

An overhead pass
Of massive concrete slabs,
Shrouding the highway,
Gives off a whiff
Of some sultry, sacrificial megalith.

Interconnecting roads, laid out like lattice-work,
Resemble a predatory web.

Asphalt deserts stagnantly reek
Of the automobile's aggressive scent markings.

A skin-head architecture:
Tall cubic gravestones with a thousand eyes,
Spawned by the lethal dream of Autopia,
Hover beside a no-man's-land
As if they've gulped up the dead.

Sometimes a car that has seen enough action,
Lies abandoned in the street for several months,
Oddly penitent in appearance,
Its metal body gnarled and twisted.

On the outskirts of cities,
Wreckers raise up mausoleums of mouldering vehicles,
Picked clean of their inhabitants
Like Parsee Towers of Silence.

The Visitor senses the eviction of the *genius loci*
From every place the car had invaded
In the dispiriting cause of turning the world
Into an interconnected no-place-at-all.

The Visitor then takes a look into the human garage:
The petrochemical fall-out
In kitchen, bathroom and living area.

Sausage-skins? Polyvinyl dichloride.
Chewing gum? Hydrocarbon wax.
Margarine? Oleo-marge –
You might not be able to tell it from butter with your tongue
But you can with a dip-stick.

Looking for love?
Petrolatum jelly will accelerate it
With loveless haste.

Giving off fumes?
. . .Mouthwash?
Benzoic acid will take your breath away,
And your larynx as well.

Losing touch?
Benzodiazepine
Should settle your feet back on the pedals.

Losing control because those in power
Are out of touch?
CS gas and a hundred other incapacitating agents
Should see you're steered back in the right direction.

Identity crisis?
Why not change sex in mid-lane with stilboestrol
Or testosterone phenylpropionate?

In the ditch?
Tank up with meths
And sputter back on the road.

Hungry?
Butylated-hydroxy-toluene
And all the other food preservatives
Now work so well

They've diversified to accommodate human meat:
Our bodies have become so rich in prophylactics
That corpses are resisting natural decomposition –
You can keep it all together
Even though you're dead.

Salves, ointments, paints, adhesives, luggage,
Detergents, food dyes, printing inks, laminates,
Rust preventers, tiles, floorings, piping, lubricants,
Fibres, solvents, scents, soap, rainwear, plastics,
Deodorants, emulsifiers, shoe cream, photographic film,
Magnetic tape, rectal suppositories, explosives . . .
All petrochemically produced
And all owned by arachnoid oligopolies
Gushing with product enthusiasm.

Like a drink? Ethyl alcohol –
Some spirits now on the market
Never saw a grain in their lives.
Another for the road?
More appropriate than ever
If the motorist's high
Comes from a refinery not a distillery.

Oh, you don't want a Scotch? Have a beer –
Stabilised with propylene glycol alginate.
Something soft?
– A fruit flavour
Enriched by propinol . . .
Now be a good boy, drink up your juice,
Then you can play with your cars.

Even the glint in someone's eye
May be petrochemical;
And each new life is anointed
With a petrochemical by-product –
Baby oil.

Should anyone remain untouched
And refuse to have petrol pumped into every orifice,
Polyurethane foam for incendiary furniture,
Combustible acrylic for curtains and covers,
Should see that you end up in a more manageable shape.

Asphalt completes the picture,
Transforming the petrochemical rainbow
Into a giant ouroborus,
Running rings around the world
And eating its own tail.
So the Detroit warlords can jeer:
'*Look, ya miserable little eco-wimps,*
Before you go handing us the Black Spot
We couldn't take our toys off the track
Even if we wanted to.
The automobile keeps the whole friggin' show on the road –
Not to mention the road on the road . . . Vroom, vroom, vroom . . .'

Oil:
From the Sanskrit root -*il*, light,
Illumination.
And *petr*, Peter, the rock.
Thus petrol is light from the rock.

If the Chinese geomancers were right
And this earth is a living organism –
The atmosphere obviously being its breath –
Oil could pass for its digestive juices,
Its cerebro-spinal fluid,
An essential bile,

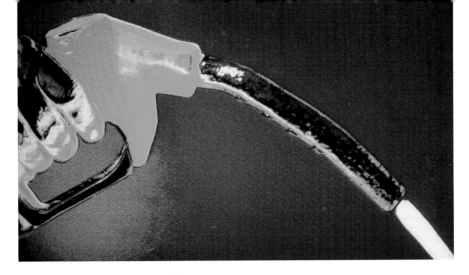

Or even its life-blood.

Before we can be illuminated
It is being burnt
By those who assuredly know best.

The global juice is fed
Through umbilical tubes
Marrying man to machine
In a miscegenating mixture.

As the earth is sucked dry, it may one day react
Against being caricatured
As a multi-barrelled Molotov cocktail,
Needled by two million bore-holes
Inserted by oil-racketeers.

Oil,
The liquefied transmutation of extinct lives:
Primordial kelp, crustacea, forminafera,
Plankton, unicellular diatoms, marine protozoa . . .
The haemins and lipids of dinosaurs
And unknown mammals from the Jurassic –
Whose first extinction was clearly not enough
For this consumer version of ancestor worship:

A sacrament
Which is most happily partaken of
When as many people as possible
Are incinerating as much of it as they can
For as trivial a reason as they can find,
To keep a continuous carousel of consumer offal on the move;
And which is most perfectly employed
Transporting convoys of layered trailers
Piled high with fresh cars.

The flagrancy of the oil's consumption
Is made more conspicuous by careless or demented spillages,
Glutinously exterminating whole populations of sea-birds

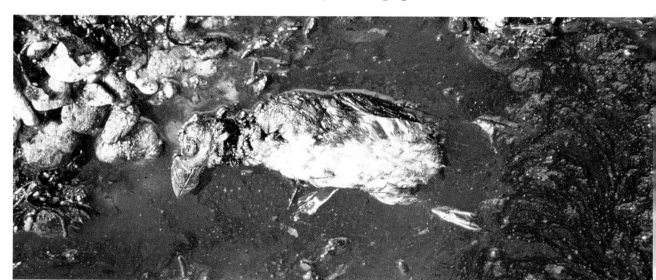

To feed gas-guzzlers with their flightless stumps of wing,
Creating a submarine sludge
That snarls up underwater life
In thousand-mile tailbacks.

The car manufacturing countries wage war over oil
And the freedom to move, on prescribed tracks.

'And the Lord made him suck oil out of the flinty rock . . .'
Deuteronomy thirty-two, verse thirteen.
Yep, this is a good ol' boys industry.
Take the gas, or nuke their ass!

Y'know there's been no basic change in auto-design
Since the flivver – the Model T?
Just featural whatnots. It's all anyone wants.
Didja know we spend twenty times as much
On tuning a car-door slam –
Getting it to say 'Well, fuck you!' or 'I'm home, honey'
As we do on safety trash?

Emphasis on safety implies accidents,
And accidents do not nurture a buyer's mood.
You're selling a daydream.

You want something that gives the moonshine an extra kick.
You're looking for the sizzle that goes with the steak.

Listen, the automobile's a credit card on wheels.
It's pushy to tell people how much you make,
So you tell 'em through your automobile,
*And you want that automobile to be **overpowering**.*
Feed people's fantasies about your success
And breed even more success.
Impress. Success.
Let safety suck.

So what's the safety lobby suggesting?
A moving padded-cell?
Listen, never mind being low on macho,
*Safety's **unsafe**.*
Because the safer it is –
With safety-belts that garrotte ya,
Pop-out windshields
And collapsible telescopic steering-columns –
None of which ever function on the day,
Bye the bye . . . by the bye bye –
The safer you feel,
And the safer you feeeeel . . .

CRASH

Wanna keep death off the roads?
Go drive on the sidewalk.
The only favours we should do safety
Is promote our cars as indestructible.

Now what are they saying?
Lead? Poison?
We got rid of it didn't we . . . ?
Though tetra-ethyl lead was a patriotic additive
Developed by the CIA
As the perfect assassination weapon:
One drop of that on your skin
And you're stone dead.

They got eight hundred tons of it
Falling on every European city every year . . . ?
Damages kids' brains? –
Just the kind of customer we wanna have in the pipe-line.

Look, why don't we concentrate on the real issues of life:
The automobile is the groundbait of civilisation.
Ask yourself why every government in the world
Trails the industry like a para-medic
And bends over backwards to winch it out of a hole . . . ?
Because it's a billion-udder milch cow.

Listen, on a good day,
Three cars are manufactured for every child born,
One per second world-wide,
And we need every kid you can manufacture
To fill 'em.

The first recorded death by an automobile
Took place on September 23rd, 1899:
A Mr H.H.Bliss stepped down from a trolley-car in New
 York City
And, while assisting a lady passenger to descend,
Was fatally struck by a horseless carriage.

The first commercially available vehicle,
A coupé, manufactured in 1899,
Was curiously christened 'My Lord'.

The Visitor pondered the results
Of submission to this lengthy test programme.

The residual husks of human glue
From rear-end collisions, whiplash collisions,
Head-on collisions, multiple collisions,
Seemed to have a cautionary value
As limp as a 'No Smoking' sticker
Slapped on to the rim of Mount Etna,
And made the Crucifixion look as if it were done
     with adhesive tape.
Rib-cages impaled by steering-columns,
Legs concertinaed in crushed doors,
Snapped bones granulated on tarmac,
Corpses kebabed by flaming upholstery,
The stomachs of pregnant women gashed open by wing-
     mirrors,
Blood-rinsed lungs punctured by door-handles,
Swatches of brain pancaked into defused slush . . .
Were all regarded as little more than traffic violations.
The acceptable face of psychopathy.

Some had almost come to regard them
In a beneficial light:
As a valued source of organs to transplant . . .
The wholeness of the human body overridden
As a pedestrian superstition.

The healing landscape,
In which the human spirit could re-tune itself,
Had been violated by a million million cars
Since the century began.
Cars' nitrogen-oxide waste,
Acting deceptively as air-borne fertiliser,
Persuaded trees it was still the growing season,
So that when winter came,
They failed to prepare for it
By turning their starches into sugar,
And froze to death;
Their tuning powers extinguished.

Their lungs – the oxygenating leaves – withered;
Pine needles grew grey, metallic tips
And dropped to the ground.
In the Black Forest miles of leafless stumps
Lay stark and joyless as a bed of nails.
In Switzerland the forests were so flimsy
Avalanches tore through them as though they were straw.

As the planet was slowly shaved of cleansing tree-cover,

Air, the Visitor observed,
Could come in as short-winded supply
As the breath of a sedentary driver.

In Rome, the traffic police went on strike,
Claiming they were unable to breathe.
In Japan, department stores were selling oxygen,
Dispensing it in purpose-built bars,
Flavoured with lime, lemon, coffee and even mushroom,
And advertising it as a sovereign remedy
For Tokyo's suffocating citizens.

The nitrous oxides,
The hydrocarbons,
The sulphur dioxide,
The carbon monoxide
Mix into a miasmic cocktail of indestructible molecules,
Feculent radicals in new and irreversible combinations –
Each year, each car belching out a quarter of a ton of it
Gift-wrapped in four tons of carbon dioxide,
Fouling up the intricate metabolism of nature.

Small signs of degradation
Appeared at first:
A rubber band
Would lose its elasticity,
Desiccate and crack;
The thread of a nylon stocking
Would wither in the street air;
Then the acid ate into paper's cellulose,
Turning it brown
As it absorbed airborne gases;
The spines of half a million books
In the British Museum, splintered and cracked,
Their bindings decayed.
Silks, cottons, brocades,
Furniture, tapestries . . .
The pigment in paintings became wizened;
Frescoes were engorged with acid
Forming corrosive blisters,
Turning the surface into a brittle crust.

Two hundred thousand tons of nitrogen dioxide
Now drop on England every year,
Reacting with all organic material.

All over Europe
The annual dosage builds up incrementally,
Forming saturating releases of nitric acid;
The copper on church roofs perishes;
Stained-glass is discoloured –
Blazing blue panes turn khaki –
The bronze horses of San Marco are swept off-stage
To give way to gimcrack facsimiles.
Marble becomes as flimsy as coral.
Joints become porous.
Arms and legs drop off.

The church bells of Europe are corroded:
Ancient, protective sounds
That once harmonised with natural events
Are now hobbled by false notes.

The Acropolis, Chartres, Rouen,
St Paul's, Lincoln, Westminster,
Notre Dame, the Statue of Liberty,
The Washington Monument, Independence Hall
Acidify, flake and rot down,
Their structures perilously eaten into:
Ornate architectural detail
Reduced to shapeless, blackened lumps
As if they had been an irrelevant distraction;
A traffic hazard.

Relics of history are obliterated
Like superfluous road-signs.

Historical memory is being re-designed
To last no longer than a recollection
Of the last service-stop.

History is to be as faceless as the present
And left for dead.

Toxic particles are then embedded into human lung
    tissue –
A more ingenious artefact,
Unsigned and priceless,
Turning invisible air
Into visible life.

The ashen metropolitan face
Betrays more than the forlorn anxieties of the market-place:
Grey is the colour of nitrous oxide poisoning.

Lungs, slowly stifled by a molecular slurry,
Are incapacitated and close down.
Useless, as worn rags in the wind.

During medical experiments at Auschwitz
Petroleum was injected into prisoners' bodies,
Just to see what would happen.
The experiment continues
With unlimited subjects.
Follow-up studies reveal
The effect to be the same:
Absorbing petrol,
Directly or indirectly,
The human body goes no faster.

Petrol's particulates seep through the skin
Like pesticides,
Leaving flesh half mummified.
Particles gnaw into the thymus gland,
Hidden behind the breast-bone,
The headquarters of the immune system,
Displacing wholesome lymphocytes
By a languid sump of distortion
With the stentorian name of lymphoblasts.
Healthy cells are bombarded into abnormality.

People on the street
Are clinically referred to by city planners
As 'pedestrian traffic',
Their lives impassively foreshortened
In an alfresco gas-chamber.

Spilt on a puddle,
Petrol is as pretty as a peacock's feather
And carries the same ill-luck:
The enticing vapour of benzene
Can bestow cancer at each sweet breath.

Children wheeled past exhaust pipes at chest level
Become catalytic converters.

The tender lining of the womb
Is considerately reinforced by lead,
Cadmium, mercury and aluminium,
Then required to filter petrol's deadly neurotoxins:
Toluene, xylene, ethylene dibromide.
Child abuse is dress-rehearsed in pregnancy.

The future is conventionally housed
Inside the womb.
But the present,
Likewise the property of the creature lying within,
Has been pitilessly clamped.

The baby is sometimes still-born
Thanks to greed's halitosis.
Breath is no longer a birthright.

While paying lip-service to clean living,
The car still aspires to peculiar paroxysms of design:

A pumping penile womb
With illuminated breasts,
And auto-erotic fuel injection
To achieve orgasmic speeds . . .
The perfect, self-satisfying body;
And the richer you are
The better body you can buy.

But, unlike musk, the odour given off
By urban man's peak experience
Is a poison.

And just as a rat with an electrode
Wired to the sex centre in its brain
Nudges the button that fires it
Again and again and again,
Neglecting hunger and thirst
Until it dies . . .
So a vapid obsession with erotic power
Stands poised to turn the planet
Into a Venusian oven:

The 'cleaner' the car, the more fuel it uses;
The more fuel it uses, the more carbon dioxide;
The more carbon dioxide, the more heat.

Despite the insidious sops of opportunist advertisers –
Whose forbears promoted cigarettes
As a cure for bronchitis –
A clean and modest car
Purchased with self-righteous complacency
Produces yet more hot air.

The 'pollution-free' car is as green as pus:
Its heat creates drought,
Killing even those
Who never aspire to a car.

Sparkling New Age morality emulates,
With the best of intentions, the psychopath
Who once climbed the tower
At the University of Austin, Texas.
He took with him three high-velocity rifles,
And a crate of ammunition,
Provisions for a long and murderous siege.
He also carried up six cases of deodorant:
He killed eleven people
While fastidiously entertaining the wish not to offend.
A mother collecting her children from school
In a car covered with worthy stickers
Expressing ecological concern
Innocently understudies Mother Kali
With her rosary of skulls.

The only green car
Is skeletally rusted and overgrown.

The Visitor then detected a yet more radical legacy:
The earth's outer skin had become attenuated,
Eaten away by humanity's totalitarian exhaust,
Forming a vast artificial anus
As large as America, as deep as Everest,
Burnt through the Southern sky,
Through which the proliferating virulence
Of ten dirty decades
Could be evacuated.

As half a billion four-wheeled spray cans
Spun carelessly round and round below
In a hazy car-lot,
With its long, hot summers,
And long, hot winters;

As cars reconditioned the air,
Usurping the elements,
Threatening to become the weather . . .
The earth's self-regulator
Had pulled the plug
And allowed the thin coat of protection
That had given humanity its life
To open up.

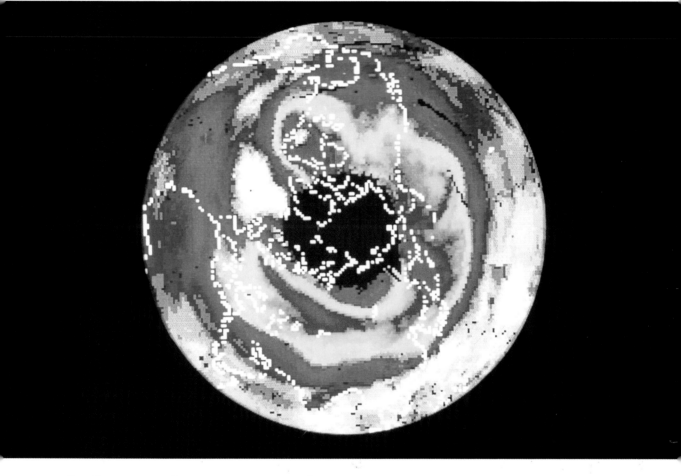

As the atmosphere was peppered
From a thousand suppurating cities,
The earth's skin was slowly leaking,
Exposing it raw to the sun . . .
Unimpressed by the self-regarding protests
Of the human race:
'But the car is so convenient.'
Or its egotistic credo:
'My journey is important. Yours isn't.'

And each autumn the orifice grows larger
As the celestial sphincter muscles grow sloppier
To allow more of the gaseous excrement to escape.

The aperture is serviced by rashes of freak storms,
Tornadoes, whirlwinds . . .
Operating like extractor fans,
Newly created by shifting layers
Of chemically heated air.

The global intelligence seemed impervious
To the human effects upon the ground:
Cataracts, skin cancers,
The stunted failure of crops
Incapable of synthesising so much ultraviolet light;
The mutant scorching of genes and DNA,
The breakdown of immunity . . .

For, as common sense would indicate,
If you were in a confined space
With half a billion cars
Remorselessly venting themselves of a noxious wind,
Someone, somewhere, would want a window open
No matter what it might bring.

Despite being swamped with artifice,
Nature still inclines to fit all phenomena
Into a larger pattern:
As cars give off their venom
Other events are homeostatically triggered.

Just as a moribund ant,
Exuding the death pheromone,
Alerts its colony to take it to the midden
For fear that they will be overrun with fungus;
So another species,
Exuding deadly pheromones,
Toys with its own extinction . . .
With an innocuous flick of an ignition key
The world can be turned off.

A second hole appears,
In the Northern hemisphere,
As if the planet were trepanning itself,
Like the ancient cure for epilepsy,
To let out low spirits,
By puncturing the skull.

Yet below,
The endless, endless flow . . .

So in love with their metal parasites
They would drive through the earth's skin,
And each as disdainful of the cost
As a cocktail-party coke-head
Snorting powdered Colombian blood.

Still curious to see how the advanced animals
Were adapting their surroundings
To suit their sense of purpose,
The Visitor observed that the fullness of the night sky
Was rarely seen or revered
By self-referential city-dwellers
Sealed off by a canopy of discoloured haze.

And noticed that the former sacred ways,
The footpaths, sunlit bridleways, lovers' lanes,
Were withered away;
Sucked dry by haemorrhaging motorways,
Dotted with civic tubs of dusty shrubs
That pass for acquaintance with nature.

Delicate arteries, once worn in by thought,
Had been displaced by swarms of carcinogenic wasps
Racing helter-skelter through chemical killing fields
On an elongated, open grave.

The Visitor scrutinised the individual drivers:
Legions of them in autistic cocoons
With an air of gloomy ferocity,
Their faces matching the expressionless landscape;

Their language confined to sultry gestures of contempt;
Worn expletives and arbitrary violence.

Two children stranded on the crash barrier
Scream at approaching cars,
Rolling their eyes away from their parents' bodies,
Mashed together in a mangled re-marriage.

Cars hiss past with mechanical disregard;
A track shoe, caught in the tail-wind,
Tumbles across the tarmac,
And comes to rest on the hard shoulder.

People die. People pass by.
Things seen at speed matter less.

Just as the ambitious cauterise compassion,
So roadside deaths are callously noted
As little more than traffic signs,
Indicating that the lives of passing drivers
Have been spared.

A man thrown from his car
Is run over, again and again,
By oncoming drivers – retarded by speed.

Drivers in Los Angeles,
Who found it irksome to be tail-gated,
Would shoot their rivals, as they overtook.
Drivers who cut into the line for gas
Were liquidated.

Even saints, in cars, became satanic,
Transmuting gold into lead:
'Come on, come on, come on.
Get out of my fucking way . . .
Can't you fucking see I want to fucking MOVE!'

Gridlocked, blocked streams of cars
Pulsate with a murderous mantra:
'Me before you. Me before you.'

All re-enacting the myth of Thrasymachus,
Who brutally defined justice
As the interests of the stronger –
Only to starve for want of bread
And hang himself.

The Visitor took a brief and sorry overview
Of a self-consuming planet,
Rotting down like an overripe puffball,
Then breezily rocketing its polluted spores into space
With boy-scout optimism,
In the lofty hope of finding some more congenial womb.

The Visitor glanced at the individual carnage,
Still mystified,
But then recalled that on a previous visit
Now extinct tribes, notably the Aztecs,
Used to sacrifice human lives,
Keeping the streets constantly lubricated
With blood
To ensure the sun would rise each day;
Their ceremonies were so extravagantly packaged
The victims glowed and shone,
And consented with pleasure.

The Visitor gazed again
At the new brand of mass execution
Casually sponsored by market forces,
And noticed that in a riot
Or a revolution
It was curious that cars,

Anyone's cars,
Always seemed the first to go.

The Visitor then glimpsed the occasional vandal,
Who, were they ever to risk losing pace
By politicising themselves,
Might feel that since no one voted for the car,
Rubbishing them required no referendum.

And that slashing tyres,
Pouring sugar into the tanks,
Shoving potatoes up the exhaust
So the pipe explodes, blowing off the manifold;
Splashing brake-fluid on to the bodywork;
Topping up the oil with valve-grinding paste;
Placing upturned nails under stationary vehicles;
Turning cars over in the street like lice
So that petrol spills out, and they can be fired . . .
Might serve to keep a few hunks of human flesh
Throbbing with life for a little longer.

It seemed to the Visitor that vandals were, perhaps,
The only experts in crisis management.

And even dogs, the Visitor observed,
Would attack the tyres of passing cars
As if biting at the tendons of a marauder.

But these, as yet, were mere midgets
Shaking their fists at the heavens . . .

For, the Visitor concluded,
If you were conceived in a car,
As many are,
If you first made love in a car,
As many have,
If you went to work in a car,
As many do,
And if you derive your sense of freedom from cars . . .
You are going to defend them
To the death.

Voices Dying to be Heard
above the Traffic

'Look at this traffic,' he said. 'Look at them, rolling along on their rubber tires in their two-ton entropy cars polluting the air we breathe, raping the earth to give their fat indolent rump-sprung American asses a free ride. Six per cent of the world's population gulping down 40 per cent of the world's oil. Hogs!' he bellowed, shaking his huge fist at the passing motorists.

'What about us?' she said.

'That's who I'm talking about.'

Edward Abbey, *The Monkey Wrench Gang*, New York: Lipincott, 1975

With all their speed forward they [automobiles] may be a step backward in civilisation – that is, in spiritual civilisation. It may be that they will not add to the beauty of the world, nor to the life of men's souls . . . almost all outward things are going to be different because of what they bring. They are going to alter war, and they are going to alter peace . . . Perhaps, ten or twenty years from now, if we can see the inward change in men by that time, I shouldn't be able to defend the gasoline engine, but would have to agree with George that automobiles 'are a useless nuisance and had no business to be invented'.

Booth Tarkington, *The Magnificent Ambersons*, New York: Doubleday, 1918

Automobilists are a picture of arrogance and wealth, with all its independence and carelessness.

Woodrow Wilson, quoted in Frank Donovan, *Wheels for a Nation*, New York: Thomas Crowell, 1965

The motorcar . . . broke up family life, or so it seemed, in the 1920s. It separated work and the domicile, as never before. It exploded each city into a dozen suburbs, and then extended many of the forms of urban life along the highway till the open road seemed to become non-stop cities. It created the asphalt jungles, and caused some 40,000 square miles of green and pleasant land to be cemented over . . .

The motorcar ended the countryside and substituted a new landscape in which the car was a sort of steeplechaser. At the same time, the motor destroyed the city as a casual environment in which families could be reared. Streets, and even sidewalks, became too intense a scene for the casual interplay of growing up. As the city filled with mobile strangers, even next-door neighbours became strangers. This is the story of the motorcar, and it has not much longer to run . . . The car, in a word, has refashioned all the spaces that unite and separate men . . .

Marshall McLuhan, *Understanding Media*, London: Routledge & Kegan Paul, 1964

Automobiles are overblown, overpriced monstrosities built by oafs to sell to mental defectives.

John Keats, *The Insolent Chariots*, New York: Lipincott, 1958

Dark was that day when Diesel
conceived his grim engine that
begot you, vile invention . . .
metallic monstrosity,
bale and bane of our Culture,
chief woe of our Commonweal.
. . . you poison
the lungs of the innocent,
your din dithers the peaceful,
and on choked roads hundreds must
daily die by chance medley

W. H. Auden, 'A Curse' from 'Thank you Fog', London: Faber and Faber, 1974

Isn't man fantastic? How did we let things get to a point where 55,000 Americans are killed in cars each year; where over 80 per cent of all air pollution is automobile induced; where our land is half-eaten by roads, parking-lots, 220,000 hideous gas stations; where traffic noise makes city streets unbearable?

Angus Black, *A Radical's Guide to Self-Destruction*, New York: Holt, Rinehart and Winston, 1971

Man's power over Nature is steadily increasing. With the aid of the atomic bomb we could literally move mountains: we could even, so it is said, alter the climate of the earth by melting the polar ice-caps and irrigating the Sahara. Isn't there, therefore, something sentimental and obscurantist in preferring bird-song to swing music and in wanting to leave a few patches of wildness here and there instead of covering the whole surface of the earth with a network of *Autobahnen* flooded by artificial sunlight?

George Orwell, *Tribune* (newspaper), London: 11 January 1946

The motorist straying off the main roads is driven by a need to escape from modern civilisation. He is a man seeking to withdraw himself, in quest, though he may not know it, of a retreat, a retreat bathed in the impalpable fragrance that is distilled by old and traditional things. He finds it, but only for a moment, for, in the act of finding it, he transforms it into something other than what he sought. It is a lane, say, leading to a village; yet scarcely has he passed that way, when the lane is widened to accommodate him. Each year the banks are cut back, the hedges trimmed, the edges tidied. Presently the native surface which reproduced the colour and characteristics of the soil disappears beneath a coat of tar, and the transformation from a lane into a road is complete. The motorists' is, indeed, the true anti-Midas touch.

C. E. M. Joad, *The Untutored Townsman's Guide to the Country*, London: Faber and Faber, 1946

I have always thought that the substitution of the internal combustion machine for the horse marked a very gloomy milestone in the progress of mankind.

Winston Churchill, *Churchill Reader, A Self-Portrait*, London: Eyre & Spottiswoode, 1954

I'd rather have a goddam horse. A horse is at least *human*, for God's sake.

J. D. Salinger, *The Catcher in the Rye*, Boston: Little, Brown, 1951

I took a great deal o' pains with his eddication, sir; let him run in the streets when he was very young, and shift for hisself. It's the only way to make a boy sharp, sir.

Sam Weller's father, in Charles Dickens, *Pickwick Papers*, London: Chapman and Hall, 1837

In the cities, apart from frightening the horses motor vehicles competed savagely with many other road users. At the end of the last century, city streets were not just transportation arteries; they served all kinds of neighbourhood and family uses. As Clay McShane has pointed out, 'push-cart vendors brought their wares to urban housewives . . . surviving lithographs and photos show great herds of children playing in the streets, generally the only open spaces.' City streets were often flanked with stalls selling all manner of produce. Musicians, conjurors, and other street entertainers provided the poor with cheap diversion. On to this seething and varied social scene, enter the motor car and exit many other performers! When the car first appeared on cinema screens in the 1890s it was often shown in the role of the bully, tipping over costers' barrows and fruit stalls; it may have been funny on the screen but it was not nearly so much fun on the streets.

Julian Pettifer & Nigel Turner, *Automania: Man and the Motor Car*, London: Collins, 1984

In the last 150 years of urbanisation, four out of five westerners, and two-fifths of the world's 5 billion population, have come to share a common space, not in the fields, but on the city's thoroughfares.

Peter Jukes, *A Shout in the Street, The Modern City*, London: Faber & Faber, 1990

All great civilisations have been based on loitering . . . Think of the Greeks, for instance. One of the most interesting adventures in our history. What were the Greeks doing in the Agora? Loitering. Not getting agoraphobia. The result is Plato.

Penelope Gilliatt (quoting Jean Renoir), 'Le Meneur de Jeu', *New Yorker*, 23 August 1969

The idea behind all the car magazines (there are about sixty in the UK alone) is that the motor car is an essential part of living . . . There is no question about who is the boss, the car or its owner – it's the car that calls the tune, all the time. One typical article asked '*Are you safe to have children?*' It put the blame for road accidents to children fair and square on the shoulders of their parents – for letting the children go on the road.

Alisdair Aird, *The Automotive Nightmare*, London: Hutchinson, 1972

For child pedestrian deaths we are among the worst in Europe, Mr Channon [Paul Channon, Secretary of State for Transport] said. A recent Gallup poll showed that 78 per cent of parents were worried that their child would be run down, yet a third of children interviewed claimed that they had been allowed to cross the road on their own from the age of seven or younger.

The Independent, London: 20 April 1989

A schoolboy knocked down by a car lay badly hurt in the road, pleading with the driver to help him. But the man took one look at him – and drove off.
 The boy, aged 15, had head injuries and a leg broken in two places. As the motorist got out to see him, he tried to stand, but collapsed in agony.
 He begged the man: 'I'm hurt. Will you get an ambulance?' But the driver ignored him, jumped back into his light-coloured Citroën car and sped off.

Daily Mirror, London: 14 January 1984

Which driver is not tempted, merely by the power of his engine to wipe out the vermin of the street, pedestrians, children and cyclists? The movements machines demand of their users already have the violent, hard-hitting, unresisting jerkiness of Fascist maltreatment.

Theodor Adorno, *Minima Moralia*, translated by E. F. N. Jephcott, London: Verso, 1978

With a Porsche, the stimulation of the senses begins with the car's appearance, it has what a Porsche designer calls 'the winning look which weapons have' . . . automobile production has often occurred in military towns which had manufacturing experience of making armaments: it is no coincidence that Turin, home of the Italian motor industry, also houses Piedmont's greatest arsenal. Similarly, André Citroën made munitions on Paris's Quai de Javel before he made cars there.

Stephen Bayley, *Sex, Drink and Fast Cars, The Creation and Consumption of Images*, London: Faber and Faber, 1986

A distinct sense of aggression is still designed into today's cars and the way in which they are marketed reinforces this symbolic aspect . . . Car names are particularly illuminating. The *Jaguar*, for example, is named after the ferocious South American beast of prey and throughout its history the styling has reflected the deadly sleekness of this successful predator. The mixture of opulence and threatening appearance has ensured it a secure niche in the market-place, appealing most to those seeking to make a strong impression. Similar connotations are evidenced in the American *Mustang*, a modern-day reminder of the feral horse of the prairies – a wild, untameable beast. Other fast and violent animals, real or imaginary, are used as designations for cars such as the *Cougar*, *Bronco*, *Panther*, *Firebird* and *Thunderbird*. The vicious hornet has also been used as a name for both American and British cars. Sharp-edged weapons constitute another group of aggressive names. In Britain the *Scimitar*, *Rapier* and *Dart* will be familiar to most people.

The important thing is that these names are not accidental. Car manufacturers go to great lengths to ensure that a particular nomenclature evokes the appropriate imagery, and consequently to sell the product. Symbols of predation, weaponry and war machines are clearly very successful in this regard.

An advertisement which appeared in *Life* magazine, for example, compared the Buick Skylark to 'a howitzer with windshield wipers . . . which is almost like having your own personal nuclear deterrent'.

The car is a weapon in the hands of those who choose to use it as such. The driver rattles his symbolic sabre and announces himself as lord of the highway. His inflated sense of confidence and his appreciation of the deadly features, both real and symbolic, transform his emotions and his behaviour. In a car, even the meekest of men has, like James Bond, a licence to kill.

Peter Marsh and Peter Collett, *Driving Passion, The Psychology of the Car*, London: Jonathan Cape, 1986

Motor-cars, some of them armoured, were run through the streets chasing the pedestrians. They ran them down and either left them mangled on the ground or crushed them to death against the walls of the houses. I saw at once that it was the long-prepared, long-awaited and long-feared war between men and machines, now at last broken out. On all sides lay dead and decomposing bodies, and on all sides, too, smashed and distorted and half-burnt motor-cars.

Herman Hesse, *Steppenwolf*, translated by Basil Creighton, London: Secker & Warburg, 1929

All Londoners know there's a close connection between driving a car and the impulse to murder.

Jane McLoughlin, *Evening Standard*, London: 8 December 1988

An international survey of moral values in 1983, conducted by Gallup International in sixteen countries, discovered that the worst crime a human being can commit is not genocide, matricide, loot, pillage or even rape, but the taking and driving away of somebody else's car without their permission. It was the only value universally shared amongst the countries surveyed.

Julian Pettifer and Nigel Turner, *Automania: Man and the Motor Car*, London: Collins, 1984

Ernest Garrad, aged 44, of Basildon, Essex, had an operation to sew his ear back on yesterday after it was bitten off when he confronted two men tampering with his neighbour's car.

The Guardian, Manchester: 3 January 1991

The car provides us with a shield and a feeling of invulnerability, a shelter for all manner of activities. We pick our noses in traffic jams, but we assume that other people cannot see us. We wind down our windows and yell at people. We make obscene gestures and threaten total strangers, behaviour we would not normally have the courage to exhibit in other circumstances. We can do all this because we feel secure in our inviolable territory.

Peter Marsh and Peter Collett, *Driving Passion, The Psychology of the Car*, London: Jonathan Cape, 1986

Timmins, a carpenter, of Forest Gate Road, Harlesden, was going home from a disco with his sister and teenage friends on Feb. 7. In Harlesden High Street he went to the aid of a girl, who had been knocked down by a car.

As he knelt by the girl, a traffic jam built up and several 'impatient' drivers tried to overtake the accident scene.

McDonald of Globe Road, Bethnal Green, was a passenger in a BMW driven by a friend who angered witnesses by trying to drive through the crowd. Timmins went up to the car and kicked it, damaging some of the chromium.

McDonald got out and stabbed Timmins in the shoulder, who died from massive internal bleeding, before reaching hospital.

Daily Telegraph, London: 9 October 1982

The figures are staggering; in 1980, the last complete year for which details are available, nearly 25,000 child pedestrians, 9,500 child cyclists, and 12,000 elderly pedestrians were killed or injured in road accidents.

The Guardian, Manchester: 1 March 1982

If we are unmindful of the Queen's highway, we shall inevitably come to clip the Queen's English and break the Queen's peace, and to the dark ages.

Charles Dickens, *Household Words*, 15 November 1856

All you need to know about American society can be gleaned from an anthropology of its driving behaviour. That behaviour tells you much more than you could ever learn from its political ideas. Drive ten thousand miles across America and you will know more about the country than all the institutes of sociology and political science put together.

Jean Baudrillard, *America*, translated by Chris Turner, London: Verso, 1989

Since June 18, there have been 30 freeway shootings, four people have been killed and several injured. Arrests have been made in three cases, but police are largely stumped by the random nature of the assaults and the ease with which the assailants melt into the traffic.

Psychologists say the perpetrators are frustrated people whose emotions are released once they are in the security of a car. A Los Angeles taxi driver had a more prosaic explanation. 'People are hearing this on the radio and saying "That sounds like a good idea. Let's shoot somebody." It's follow the leader.'

Daily Telegraph, London: 7 August 1987

Motorway madness is reaching new levels of intensity . . . last week in Britain a driver told how he was ambushed in his BMW while travelling in the outside lane of the M4. He was beaten up by other motorists who wanted to overtake.

According to Roy Bailey, the consulting psychiatrist to Drivers International, whose instructors teach advanced driving technique, these incidents arise because of the vast quantities of information which flash before the eyes of a motorist travelling at high speed.

This flow of information – including the positions of other cars, the scenery, the data on the dashboard – is so rapid that drivers will often not realise how much they are taking in and responding to.

However, the speed and amount of work their minds and bodies are doing while driving cause motorists to become highly stressed as they secrete the type of blood chemicals which promote alertness.

After driving for long periods a driver may become hyper-aroused, and Bailey says this 'starts to put the body and mind under such pressure that people are liable to revert to very primitive behaviour'.

Neville Hodgkinson, 'Mad drivers in fast lanes', *Sunday Times*, London: 28 February 1988

Headlights themselves are potential triggers for aggressive encounters. Even the most passive of drivers is likely to become enraged by oncoming cars with undipped lights. Blazing headlights certainly impair forward vision and are distinctly uncomfortable. But this is not the whole reason why people become angry. The bright headlamps are the automotive equivalent of the hostile stare. Fixed, wide-open gaze has a long evolutionary history as a signal of hostility. It is used by chimpanzees eager to climb up, or to defend their position in the dominance hierarchy. In human cultures it serves exactly the same function. 'Looking daggers' is an apt description of this feature of non-verbal communication. In the case of the automobile, however, 'looks' can literally kill. The car with the lights at full beam is a hostile stranger in the night – an immediate threat which arouses primordial fears and gears us up for retaliation. Recently, one British driver was so angered by the undipped lights of another car that he immediately turned round and pursued the offender. Having caught up with him and forced him to stop, he proceeded to smash all the lights on the car with a jack handle.

Peter Marsh and Peter Collett, *Driving Passion, The Psychology of the Car*, London: Jonathan Cape, 1986

Gun terror has returned to Southern California's highways, sparking fears of a new round of violence on Los Angeles roads similar to that seen last year.

Police said a car pulled up alongside 23-year-old Juan Trujillo as he drove along the Santa Ana freeway yesterday and a man opened fire with an assault rifle, killing him. A California highway patrol officer said: 'One incident like this is all you need to start the whole cycle again.' He said that the authorities could do 'little more than keep our fingers crossed'.

Police fear it may spark a new spate of killings like those early last year when there were more than 50 incidents of gun-carrying motorists venting their anger and frustration. At least five people died and 10 were wounded, and many motorists refused to venture on the freeways.

Evening Standard, London: 7 August 1989

A driver who ran down and killed a hitch-hiker who gave him a 'V' sign for failing to give him a lift, was sentenced to five years' youth custody at Bristol Crown Court yesterday.

The court was told that Dalley mounted the pavement and drove his van at almost 50 mph into Mr Clifford James, an able seaman in the Royal Navy . . .

Daily Telegraph, London: 30 July 1988

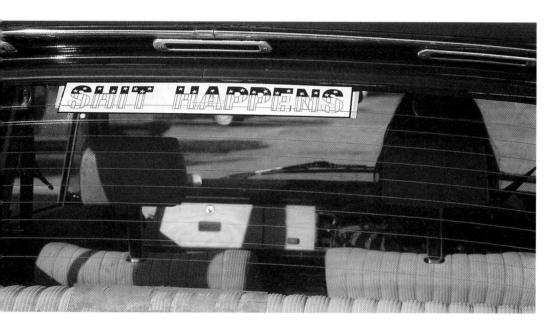

The most typical triumph of mass production today, the motor car, has, since 1900, statistics show, slaughtered vastly more human beings than have been killed in *all* the wars ever fought by the United States – while the total number of those injured or maimed is probably much higher.

So two generations have grown up for whom every variety of mindless violence has become the constant accompaniment to 'civilised' life, sanctified by other equally debased but modish customs and institutions.

Lewis Mumford, *The Pentagon of Power*, New York: Harcourt Brace, 1970

Mexico City is extremely large. Exhausted by the altitude and suffocated by the pollution, I found my resolve to work my way through it weakening day by day. Anyway it was Holy Week. The newspapers were full of the impending holiday carnage. *Already – 1,350 accidents. 152 dead!!* In a country where children are given little chocolate skeletons as a *memento mori*, the bank holidays have a special entertainment value.

Patrick Marnham, 'Holy Week', *Granta*, Cambridge: Issue 10, 1984

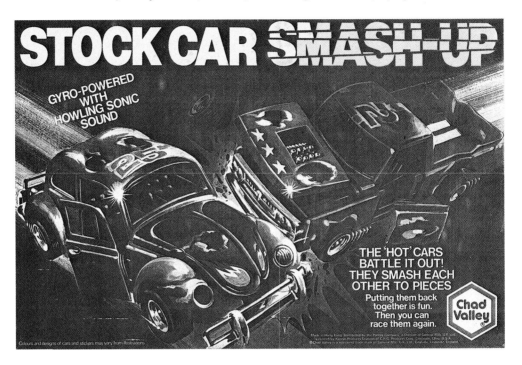

At least 20 cars ran over a 12-year-old girl as she sought help for her dying father after a motorway crash, police said yesterday. A motorist finally called the police, who found the girl's remains spread over 50 yards.

The Guardian, Manchester: 16 November 1988

A man was knocked down and killed in a main street in Camborne by 'a piece of blatant and reckless driving', it was alleged yesterday.

Michael Mounce was hit by a van as he stood in the middle of a street and carried for several yards before he fell from the vehicle, claimed Mr Anthony Donner, prosecuting.

The van driver, —————, looked back and 'appeared to laugh and then drove off at a very fast speed', added Mr Donner at Bodmin Crown Court.

Western Morning News, Plymouth: 22 May 1986

Stories abound of astonishingly mild sentences for America's 'socially accepted form of murder'. A Wisconsin man who ran down and killed a child was given a $284 fine. The killer of a 15-year-old boy got two years' probation, a $200 fine and lost his licence for 16 months.

William Scobie, *The Observer*, London: 12 September 1982

A motorist involved in a fatal accident was found guilty of driving without due care and attention by Callington magistrates on Thursday and fined £40.

Cornish Times, Liskeard: 4 May 1984

I n a darkened surveillance center alongside Interstate 45, I scanned fourteen TV screens that monitor a key six and a half-mile section of the road. Nearby, a computer whirrs and clicks, automatically analysing the traffic. Sensing gaps in the pattern, the computer actuated signals regulating the flow of incoming vehicles from freeway entrance ramps.

Suddenly, on one of the TV screens, I saw a car veer out of control, smash into a lamp post, and burst into flames. 'Accident on camera 7!' a technician called. Beside him, a police officer snatched up a telephone and issued swift instructions. Soon a fire truck flashed onto the screen, followed by an ambulance and a police car.

Once upon a time an accident would have stalled the commuters for hours. Now, mere minutes elapsed before the massed autos resumed their inexorable flow.

R. P. Jordan, 'Our growing Interstate Highway system', *National Geographic*, February 1968

I magine that on BBC Breakfast Time there was an interview with the three people who were going to be killed that morning on the M4. Motorists are asked to avoid using the M4 to prevent the deaths of these people. What would happen?

Edward de Bono, *The Guardian*, Manchester: 5 September 1990

More people were killed on Soviet roads in 1988 (49,486) than died during the nine-year Soviet presence in Afghanistan.

New Internationalist, California: May 1989

More than a quarter of a million people are killed every year in road accidents in the Third World. Of those who die between the ages of five and 44, 10 per cent are killed in accidents, a higher proportion than from any disease listed in the World Health Organisation's statistics.

Accidents on the roads are costing the developing countries more than £15 billion a year. Most third world States suffer a greater financial loss from these accidents than they receive in foreign aid.

The Observer, London: 12 December 1982

Gruesome statuary adorns the principal thoroughfares of São Paulo, to remind drivers that though the Grand Prix championship still eludes Brazil, the country has taken the prize for the world's highest death-rate in traffic accidents.

'I was late for work,' reads the inscription under a horribly pancaked saloon raised on a decorative plinth to sober the city's impatient motorists. At a nearby junction, mangled pieces of motor bike are ignored by riders who thread through the traffic with helmets dangling from their arms like shopping bags. Seat-belts are considered such a European eccentricity that an attempt to enforce their use 18 months ago was quickly abandoned. Ignoring traffic-lights and drunken driving were the main causes of the 640,000 road accidents last year in Brazil, in which 60,000 people died and 350,000 were injured. This year the death toll may be double, because the Transport Ministry had recorded 500,000 accidents by last month.

Sunday Times, London: 30 July 1988

The automobile laconically runs down pedestrians. It gnaws into the side of a barn or else, grinning, it flies down a slope. It can't be blamed for anything. Its conscience is as clear as Monsieur Citroën's conscience. It only fulfils its destiny: It is destined to wipe out the world.

Ilya Ehrenburg, *The Life of the Automobile*, first published in Russian by Petropolis Verlag, Berlin, 1929; translated by Joachim Neugroschel, London: Pluto Press, 1985

My 17-year-old son was killed one year ago in a collision . . . After Tristan died, I saw the roads of Britain swimming in blood. They will stay like that because until it happens to you, you are happy to be part of the conspiracy of silence. And after it has, you are one of the quietly suffering who don't have enough strength left to try to change the world.

Susanne MacGregor, Letter to *The Guardian*, Manchester: 4 January 1988

Once out of curiosity, I began counting beer cans that had been tossed into a ditch from passing cars. The score was more than 350 in a mile.

John Perry, *Our Polluted World*, New York: F. Watts, 1967

A college lecturer drank two and a half bottles of vodka before he mowed down and killed a boy, a court heard yesterday. George Clark left Jonathan Parfitt, 13, dead on the pavement and drove on to buy his fourth bottle of the day.

Daily Express, London: 27 March 1990

One in four drivers killed on the streets of New York City is known to have taken cocaine in the previous 48 hours and well over half had taken cocaine or alcohol.
  Dr Peter Marzuk and colleagues from Cornell University Medical College reviewed nearly 1,000 deaths between 1984 and 1987. They believe that as users say they feel hyper-alert and euphoric after taking the drug they are likely to take more risks.

The Independent, London: 16 January 1990

I know of one long-term user [of heroin] who drives an ambulance for a living. I called to visit his wife one day at around 2 pm in time to see the ambulance pull up outside. He staggered out, barely able to stand, and told me, in slurred speech, that a social worker friend had shared some heroin, leaving him too stoned to drive. He had somehow managed to get home and had written off work for the rest of the day, leaving the ambulance where it stood, right outside his house.

Tam Stewart, 'The battle to be normal', Real Lives, London: *New Statesman*, 2 October 1987

One out of every five drivers falls asleep at the wheel and at least 40,000 traffic accidents a year are thought to be sleep-related . . . They say that in get-ahead America people think sleeping eight hours a night indicates a lack of drive and ambition.

'Dermot Purgavie's America', *Daily Mail*, London: 16 May 1990

The traffic light showed red, when the 70-year-old driver in Moers (Lower Rhine) suffered a deadly heart-attack. After his foot had slipped off the brake pedal, the car with automatic transmission started moving and ran over two little girls, aged seven.

'Toter überfuhr zwei Kinder' [Dead man ran over two children], *Hamburger Abendblatt*, Hamburg: 25 June 1987

Drivers involved in accidents have a greater tendency than other motorists to describe themselves as better-than-average drivers. In a survey carried out for a motor insurance company half of those interviewed said television programmes influenced the way people drove, and nearly a third thought television influenced people to drive more dangerously.

Colin Dryden, 'Drivers who think they are better than others', *Daily Telegraph*, London: 3 October 1989

A few years back a driving researcher named L. Black did an interesting study. He interviewed a cross-section of motorists who agreed that cars should be designed with safety as their single most important feature. The motorists talked about various technical designs that would serve this purpose; for instance, they thought automatic seat belts were a wonderful idea. Overall, accidents made them very nervous indeed. Safety should come first – at least that is what they said.

Black then hypnotised each of these people, and the second set of interviews yielded quite different results. Safety was no longer the central issue. They now felt that a well-designed automobile was one that was sleek, low, and fast! Slow drivers were the ones who caused accidents. The hypnotised drivers now agreed that the greatest aspect of driving was the feeling of power and mastery of being behind the wheel!

K. T. Berger, *Zen Driving*, New York: Ballantine, 1988

Taking all the death statistics available in the United States from 1900 through to 1975 . . . we find that mortality rates from suicide, homicide and motor accidents parallel one another very closely over time: when the suicide rate rises, so does the rate of dying from accidents.

Richard Totman, *Mind, Stress and Health*, London: Souvenir Press, 1990

A bereaved woman who sparked a major police operation after driving erratically up the M5 at speeds of 110 mph was recovering in a psychiatric hospital last night.

The 21-year-old Honiton woman, who had just heard that her boyfriend had died unexpectedly, was chased by police helicopter and patrol cars through Mid-Devon before overturning her BMW car at Thorverton. Police believe deep distress led her to lose control of her car.

Western Morning News, Plymouth: 18 August 1990

I was in an emotional situation that I found impossible to resolve. Any resolution, even if I could have thought of one, was effectively blocked.

Given the irresponsibility of being in a car in such an emotional and alcoholic state, I was fortunate not to involve anyone else in the inevitable accident. In such a state it was as if the problem was out of my hands. After having demolished a central island, the car came to rest upside down. I was pulled from under the car with a graze on each shin and a small mark above the bridge of the nose where I had hit the steering wheel.

I was taken into a basement gambling club, given some black coffee and after a short time, left.

I looked across the road at the car and thought, oh, someone must have had an accident, hailed a taxi and went home.

I slept well and woke up elated. All emotional tension and attachment had been dissipated.

Terry Stewart, in a personal communication to Heathcote Williams, October 1990

In Austria, which has the third highest suicide rate in Europe, police estimate that around 50 motorists a year deliberately kill themselves whilst driving. This estimate, however, is based only on those cases where suicidal tendencies were known to exist in the first place. More detailed research at the University of California, gives us good reason to suppose that a significant proportion of single-vehicle crashes are, in fact, intentional suicides.

Peter Marsh and Peter Collett, *Driving Passion, The Psychology of the Car*, London: Jonathan Cape, 1986

By the end of this century a quarter of a million people will have been killed on the roads of the UK . . . This is of course a world-wide scourge. In the world as a whole traffic kills about 200,000 people a year – one almost every two and a half minutes . . . in 1969, the total road-deaths toll since the first car took to the road in the United States reached two million.

Alisdair Aird, *The Automotive Nightmare*, London: Hutchinson, 1972

Persons killed or injured in road traffic accidents:

	Killed	Injured
AUSTRIA 1988	1,446	57,843
BELGIUM 1988	1,967	84,851
CYPRUS 1988	103	4,345
CZECHOSLOVAKIA 1988	1,464	4,345
DENMARK 1988	713	11,790
FINLAND 1988	653	11,909
FRANCE 1988	10,548	244,042
GERMAN DEMOCRATIC REPUBLIC 1988	1,649	39,521
FEDERAL REPUBLIC OF GERMANY 1988	8,213	448,223
GREECE 1988	1,511	29,370
HUNGARY 1988	1,706	27,776
ICELAND 1988	29	898
IRELAND 1987	462	8,409
ITALY 1988	6,784	217,511
LUXEMBOURG 1988	84	1,863
MALTA 1988	9	728
NETHERLANDS 1988	1,366	47,981
NORWAY 1988	378	10,962
POLAND 1988	2,534	43,626
PORTUGAL 1988	2,534	59,532
ROUMANIA 1988	1,191	5,173
SPAIN 1988	6,348	164,949
SWEDEN 1988	813	22,838
SWITZERLAND 1988	945	30,083
TURKEY 1987	7,530	80,321
UNITED KINGDOM 1987	5,339	316,070
YUGOSLAVIA 1988	4,555	60,837
EUROPE – Total 1988	71,100	1,978,000
UNITED STATES 1980	51,091	3,410,000

Economic Commission for Europe (Geneva), *Statistics of Road Traffic Accidents in Europe*, New York: United Nations Publications, Vol. XXXV, 1990

Nancy Cruzan, now 32, has done nothing for the past seven years. She has not hugged her mother or gazed out of the window or played with her nieces. She has neither laughed nor wept, nor spoken a word. Since her car crashed on an icy night, she has lain so still for so long, her hands have curled into claws; nurses wedge napkins under her fingers to prevent the nails piercing her wrists. But her parents are suffering. It is they who live with her living death.

Nancy Gibbs, 'Love and Let Die', *Telegraph Magazine*, London: 28 April 1990

In his book [Norman R. Bernstein, *Emotional Care of the Facially Disfigured*, Boston: Little, Brown, 1976] Norman Bernstein tells the story of Robert C., who was burned in a car accident at the age of 21. He was a hitchhiker, a soldier going home on leave, and when the car he was riding in crashed into a semi truck, he was thrown clear of the wreckage. He ran into the flames and pulled the driver out, a hero. The driver died, and Robert was deeply burned on the arms and face. He lost eight fingers, both ears, his nose, his eyelids, and almost all his facial skin and hair. Bernstein shows us a picture of Robert midway through his recovery. He is minimalist, taut. His eyes are too large, too wet, unframed by lids and lashes. The eye globes seem to bulge out of the white face. His nose is two holes, a little bloody . . .

   'Each person who looked at Robert had to make an effort to think of him as a human being. Some children have come up to him when he was sitting in a car and asked 'what he was' and how he came to look that way. While he was visiting a friend's house, a teenage girl walked into the room and saw him. She said what a horrible-looking mask he was wearing and tried to remove it.' Robert lives with his parents, who care for him like a toddler because of his lost fingers.

Sallie Tisdale, 'Burning', *Whole Earth Review*, Sausalito, California: No. 50, Spring 1986

A farm worker was so upset over the injuries suffered by a family in a crash with his pick-up truck that he grabbed a shotgun and killed himself.

Daily Mirror, London: 4 August 1981

A budget car had been booked for me. The form had a big red disclaimer stamped on it: 'Kangaroo damage will be charged to lessee.' A mite unfair, I thought, because once a kangaroo decides to contest the right-of-way, a driver really has no choice but to hit it, because a kangaroo on the hop is longer than the road is wide. Aim at either side and you will clip nose or tail and the rest of the creature will swing round and bang into the side of the car.

   A wounded animal is doomed to die of gangrene in agony in the pitiless sun, so it is country practice to aim directly at the beast and kill it fair and square. For this purpose vehicles are fitted with roo bars which keep the big animal from coming through the windscreen. Correct procedure is to reverse back and check that the animal is dead, and then to lug it off the road.

Germaine Greer, 'How to Crash into a Kangaroo', *The Observer*, London: 8 August 1982

Speed limits in the New Forest are to be cut from 60 mph to 40 mph in a one-year experiment starting today. Last year, 124 of the forest's wild ponies were killed in road accidents and dozens more were injured.

The Guardian, Manchester: 19 March 1990

One of the animal 'guinea-pigs' at the ONSER research laboratory in Lyons, France, is strapped into position before a simulated road crash. Since it opened in 1971 the research establishment has used some 31 baboons and 26 pigs, as well as human corpses.

London: Camera Press, 30955–5

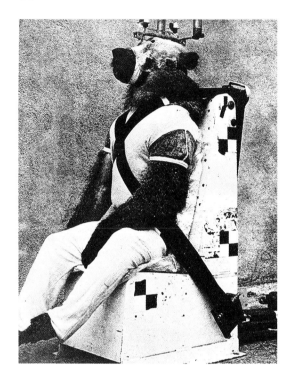

Germans regard themselves as animal-lovers. Every second individual is a pet-owner, but on the roadside we eradicate animals with our cars – hunting on wheels, but hardly anyone takes any notice of their dying. Road-cleaners remove their little bodies early in the morning. Cleanliness has been restored . . . On a Sunday in July 1985 we counted the number of dead animals on a stretch of country road one hundred kilometres long. There were thirteen birds, three cats and seventeen hedgehogs; thirty-three animals killed. We did not count butterflies, beetles or other insects stuck to radiator grilles or windows or squashed by tyres.

Peter M. Bode, Sylvia Hamberger and Wolfgang Zängl, *Alptraum Auto* [*Car Nightmare*, unpublished translation by Elke Cann], Munich: Raben Verlag, 1986

So mechanical man in triumph seated upon the seat of his machine will be driven mad from within himself, and sightless . . .

D. H. Lawrence, 'The Triumph of the Machine', *The Complete Poems of D. H. Lawrence*, vol. II, London: Heinemann, 1964

Remember this, the spirit of a man resides in his ears; when he hears what is agreeable to him, the pleasure diffuses itself over all his body; but when the contrary happens he is anxious and uneasy.

Herodotus, *c.*480–*c.*425 BC, *Collected Works*, 'Polymnia XXXIX', translated from the Greek by the Rev. William Beloe, London: Luke Hansard & Sons, 1812

It is possible that the hearing of the population as a whole has begun to be affected by the rise in ambient noise in cities through the growth of mechanisation in transport.

British Medical Journal, 11 September 1965

Donald Appleyard, an urban planner, and Mark Lintell, an architect, investigated the effects of traffic noise on the residents of three streets in a middle-income San Francisco neighbourhood. People on the noisiest street reported that it was a rather lonely place to live, while those on the quietest one perceived it as a friendly and sociable area.

Sheldon Cohen, 'Sound Effects on Behaviour', *Psychology Today*, New York: October 1981

Is the roar of city traffic, always there by day and night, perhaps the reason why headaches now seem to have become so much a part of Western civilisation?

Alisdair Aird, *The Automotive Nightmare*, London: Hutchinson, 1972

People may well drive less safely because of the noise to which they are subject. Experiments have shown that, in an army troop-carrier, the more noise and vibration people are exposed to, the longer it takes them to respond to 'random obscure signals' – the sort of things drivers have to spot and act on immediately, for safety.

M. Loeb and G. Jeanthieu, 'The influence of noxious environmental stimuli on vigilance', *Journal of Applied Psychology* 42, 47–9, 1958

One curious effect is that it can upset people's vision. Experiments in France [I. Grognot and G. Perdriel, 'Influence of noise on certain visual functions', *Vision Research*, November 1961] showed that when people were exposed to a noise level of over 90 decibels for the very short time of five to ten minutes, they became less good at judging distances, tended to see colours somewhat differently, and became much less good at seeing in the dark. Good vision is vital to drivers: it is alarming that high noise levels can distort it – and that long-distance lorry-drivers, hurtling through the night at the wheel of their twenty and thirty-tonners, may literally be blinded by the din in their cabs.

Alisdair Aird, *The Automotive Nightmare*, London: Hutchinson, 1972

The Environmental Protection Agency estimates that more than 70 million Americans now live in neighbourhoods with noise levels high enough to interfere with communication and to cause annoyance and dissatisfaction.

Sheldon Cohen, 'Sound Effects on Behaviour', *Psychology Today*, New York: October 1981

Tests on Mabaans, who live a quiet life in the Ethiopian highlands, have shown that even when they are in their seventies, they have better hearing than typical American city dwellers in their thirties.

P. Beales, 'Modern Noise', *Hearing*, February 1969

Noise made by a teenager's souped-up car so irritated a neighbour, his wife and their 21-year-old son that they paid two men $2,000 Canadian (£886) to kill him, police alleged yesterday at Valleyfield, Quebec. Mr Remi Lahaie, 19, was found shot, strangled with wire, stabbed 14 times, and with his throat slit. All five have been charged with murder.

'Car noise led to death contract', *Daily Telegraph*, London: 1 February 1988

After almost a week [in São Paulo] Tawapuh pulled my face close to his own, and looking sadly into my eyes, very quietly said 'How could you return to this world after seeing how we live? How can you breathe this foul air or sleep with these terrible noises?'

Orlando and Claudio Villas Boas, *Xingu: The Indians, Their Myths*, New York: Farrar, Straus, 1973

True silence . . . is to the spirit, what sleep is to the body, nourishment and refreshment.

William Penn, 1644–1718

The automobile is the idol of the modern age . . . The man who owns a motorcar gets for himself, besides the joys of touring, the adulation of the walking crowd, and the daring driver of a racing machine that bounds and rushes and disappears in the perspective in a thunder of explosions is a god to the women.

George Dupuy, 'The Conquering Automobile', *The Independent* (London), 12 April 1906, cited in James T. Flink, *America Adopts the Automobile, 1890–1914*, Cambridge, Mass: MIT Press, 1975

This tiny island [Guernsey], where the speed of motor cars is limited to 35 mph probably has more Porsches per capita than anywhere else in the UK. They can never be driven at a fraction of the dynamic potential which engineers have struggled to build into them. These powerful cars are not transport, they are aphrodisiacs. They are sold as costumes and worn for sexual display.

Stephen Bayley, *Sex, Drink and Fast Cars, The Creation and Consumption of Images*, London: Faber and Faber, 1988

A girl aged 11 was killed when a motorist attempted a 'racing driver' turn at a sharp bend, the Old Bailey was told yesterday. The red Lotus Esprit spun across a grass verge and struck Helen Morris as she rode a bicycle on the pavement. She was thrown over a hedge and died soon afterwards.

The Independent, London: 17 July 1990

We value speed more highly than we value human life. Then why not say so, instead of every few years having one of these hypocritical campaigns (at present it is 'Keep Death off the Roads' – a few years back it was 'Learn the Kerb Step'), in the full knowledge that while our roads remain as they are, and present speeds are kept up, the slaughter must continue?

George Orwell, 'As I Please', *Tribune* (newspaper), London: 8 November 1946

A woman coming between a man and his car is risking her life.

– The Rt Hon Barbara Castle, Secretary of State for Transport

Spontaneous ejaculation, apparently, is the occupational hazard of motor racing: a man's love affair with his car is serious stuff. Or so says Keith Botsford, the former motor racing editor of the Sunday Times . . . Although only one racing driver has ever admitted to him that he had an orgasm on getting into his car for the first time, Botsford is convinced that stained jump-suits are far from uncommon on the Grand Prix circuits of the world. The confession does more than bring a new meaning to the cliché, 'the thrills and spills of motor racing.'

Bill O'Neill, 'Lifting the bonnet on motor cars', *New Scientist*, London: 18 August 1988

It is not sheer accident that Cadillac stylists speak of the 'bosoms' on their bumpers, or that Madison Avenue applauded the Edsel for its 'vaginal' look, or that so many Detroit stylists lavish so much attention on the rear ends of automobiles.

John Keats, *The Insolent Chariots*, New York: Lipincott, 1958

I could bring myself to orgasm simply by thinking of the car in which we performed our sexual acts.

J. G. Ballard, *Crash!*, London: Jonathan Cape, 1973

Two generations of Americans know more about the Ford coil than the clitoris, about the planetary system of gears than the solar system.

John Steinbeck, *Cannery Row*, New York: Viking Press, 1945

The American really loves nothing but his automobile.

William Faulkner, *Intruder in the Dust*, New York: Random House, 1948

A few years back, I attended a public debate between the founder of a renowned world-saving organisation and the CEO of a coal-mining company. The Bad Guy won the toss, took the mike and said to the large audience of obviously hostile adults, 'Before we start, I'd like to know how many of you would be willing to give up your automobiles right now.' A loud cheer went up, most hands waving madly in the affirmative. The miner stared maybe a full minute, waiting for the tumult to subside. Then he said quietly, with just a hint of a sneer in his voice, 'I'm not about to waste an evening talking to a roomful of liars.' And then he walked out.

He had our number. Though we may like to appear eco-chic, we are not about to give up cars, nor will folks in developing countries give up their dream of owning a car.

J. Baldwin, 'Eco-Cars', *Whole Earth Review*, Sausalito, California: No. 68, 1990

The greatest shame for a grown man is to admit he cannot drive a car.
'Motoring', *Sunday Times Magazine*, London: 18 February 1990

There is a maxim that to be seen on a bus after the age of forty is a sign of failure.

Alice Thomas Ellis, *More Home Life*, London: Duckworth, 1987

Something I've learned is that whatever else happens, people cannot bear to go without a 'new' car in the drive. They might be eating sardines every night indoors but outside they've got an emblem of prosperity.

Brian Grant (managing director of *Exchange and Mart*), *Weekend Guardian*, Manchester: 17–18 March 1990

Congratulations! You have won the chance to pay just £360,000 for the car of your dreams. So said a letter sent last week to 350 of the world's richest motorists . . . Although Jaguar is still building the prototype, more than 1,300 people from 40 countries put down a £50,000 deposit on the untested car; for every successful applicant there were three failures . . . The applicants are rumoured to have included Mick Jagger, Elton John and Petula Clark.

One rock musician who has won an option on the car, is Nick Mason, the drummer with Pink Floyd. Mason, who plans to use the Jaguar to drive between race meetings in Europe, said he would have been 'suicidally depressed' if he had been rejected by Jaguar.

Ian Birrell, 'Select few pounce on Jaguar supercar', *Sunday Times*, London: 4 March 1990

It's fashionable now to issue demands for people themselves to change their life-styles. But will they? I don't know people from the openly selfish party, but over the weekend I took a sample of opinion from the party which used to argue that only socialism could achieve green ends. A young activist on the Labour left told me that he relentlessly drove his car everywhere, and 'would drive it to the toilet if he could'. He dismissed concern about the greenhouse effect as a moral panic among the white middle class who resented ordinary people being able to afford cars and join them in clogging up and polluting the roads. In quiet despair, I tried this out later on a more middle-of-the-road party member: 'You know, there's some truth in that.'

Vicky Hutchings, 'Some like it hot', *New Statesman*, London: 1 June 1990

Every newsreel showed Hitler being driven through cheering crowds in his six-wheeler Mercedes-Benz. Once in my life, I have ridden in one. It was a taxi from Ipswich. I asked the driver why he had chosen so opulent and expensive a vehicle for such a workaday job. 'Because I'll always get my money back,' he explained. 'People have this superstition that there's something special about a Merc.'

Colin Ward, 'Fringe Benefits', *New Statesman*, London: 4 August 1989

In 1981 during a visit to the Vatican's private garage where he talked to drivers employed by the Holy See, Pope John Paul said:

> Your profession as chauffeurs should remind you constantly that we are all on the road, heading at high speed towards eternity. It should teach you that a car, to work well, should be looked after with constant loving care just like our soul, immortal and redeemed by Christ, along the road to salvation [*Standard*, Niagara Falls: 6 January, 1981].

Lyall Watson, *The Nature of Things*, London: Hodder & Stoughton, 1990

WORLD'S HIGHEST STANDARD OF LIVING

There's no way like the American Way

We Americans hardly need to ponder a mystery that has troubled men for millennia: what is the purpose of life? For us, the answer will be clear, established, and for all practical purposes indisputable: the purpose of life is to produce and consume automobiles.

Jane Jacobs, *The Death and Life of Great American Cities*, London: Jonathan Cape, 1962

Take it for granted that nobody, not even a genius, can guarantee that your car won't fall apart five minutes after he's examined it.

Henry Miller, 'The Air-Conditioned Nightmare', *New Directions*, 1945

There had been a series of rear-end collisions [involving the Pinto] resulting in fuel tank explosions, causing other fatalities and leading to other lawsuits. *Mother Jones*, a small left-wing magazine, made national headlines by charging that 'secret documents' revealed that the design problems which made the Pinto especially susceptible to explosion and fire had been known to the team developing the car. During the Gray-Grimshaw trial a confidential company memo was introduced into evidence showing that Ford was fully aware of what might happen to the Pinto. The author of the document estimated that 180 people could die as a result of the Pinto's defects during the life span of the car, and another 180 be seriously burned. These deaths and injuries, the analyst calculated, had potential 'social costs' of $49.5 million compared to the $137 million it would cost to fix the Pinto immediately. Thus the modification would not be 'cost effective'.

Peter Collier and David Horowitz, *The Fords, An American Epic*, London: Collins, 1988

Poor workmanship and inadequate inspection is also much cheaper for the manufacturer than the cost of a good job well done. Cars now leave the factory in such a bad state that about 15 to 25 per cent of a garage's time is spent on putting right faults left by the manufacturers [Motor Industry, 2.70].

Alisdair Aird, *The Automotive Nightmare*, London: Hutchinson, 1972

The trouble with most forms of transport . . . is basically one of them not being worth all the bother. On Earth – when there had been an Earth, before it was demolished to make way for a new hyperspace bypass – the problem had been with cars. The disadvantages involved in pulling lots of black sticky slime from out of the ground where it had been safely hidden out of harm's way, turning it into tar to cover the land with, smoke to fill the air with and pouring the rest into the sea, all seemed to outweigh the advantages of being able to get more quickly from one place to another – particularly when the place you arrived at had probably become, as a result of this, very similar to the place you had left; i.e. covered with tar, full of smoke and short of fish.

Douglas Adams, *The Restaurant at the End of the Universe*, London: Pan, 1980

In one year the United States burns in its automobiles more petroleum than the Alaskan oil field accumulated in 100,000 years.

Robert Ornstein and Paul Ehrlich, *New World New Mind*, London: Methuen, 1989

Drilling a well's a gamble. The payoff can be real big, or you can go broke in a hurry. The payoff can be terrible when men's lives are lost. You can take every precaution but you never know when something will let go. It can happen any time. It can happen any place. Sure as hell, it'll happen again, but then that's the romance of oil.

Philip Singerman, *Red Adair, An American Hero*, London: Bloomsbury, 1989

The price of oil is paid mostly in dollars but also in blood. This is not only true of the Gulf. Since the end of the slave trade, no other energy resource has cost so much in human suffering and death. That price has been paid lavishly – and for the most part unnecessarily – in the North Sea, where the oil workers went on strike again last week.

Neal Ascherson, *The Independent on Sunday*, London: 12 August 1990

The fire in the last of the burning oil wells under the Piper Alpha platform has been put out, more than three weeks after the North Sea disaster. The task of finding the bodies of the 124 of the 167 oilmen killed in the gas explosion will begin shortly.

The Independent, London: 30 July 1988

Oil spills threaten marine life long after the event. Even now, the remnants of pollution from the Amoco Cadiz, wrecked in March 1978, are interfering with the reproduction of fish around the coast of Brittany.

Since the wreck, biologists have kept a close watch on local marine life. In 1978, the plaice did not grow properly, their fins bore lesions and many did not breed. T. Brule of the Laboratory of Animal Biology at the University of Western Brittany in Brest, finds that plaice are still developing with abnormal reproductive organs. Some had empty egg follicles; and some had masses of connective tissue and blood vessels rather than reproductive cells. The sediments of estuaries where the plaice live remain contaminated.

'Oil pollution lingers longer', *New Scientist*, London: 21 May 1987

The area of the spill [from the Exxon Valdez] is so remote and the beaches are so inaccessible that almost no animals affected by the oil have been found so far. Few may ever be found because of the difficulties. Those that are recovered alive have only a small chance of survival.

In the pristine paradise for birds, fish and animals that was Prince William Sound in south-central Alaska before the Exxon tanker spilled 12 million gallons of crude, the saddest victims will be the sea otters. These playful animals' luxurious fur was once so regarded that at the turn of the century they were nearly extinct. They are now protected.

Other mammals threatened by the 100-square-mile slick now dumping inches-thick goo on five small islands in the inlet are seals, sea-lions, killer whales, and porpoises. Dozens of varieties of sea and shore birds live here. Fish such as salmon, herring, and crabs, shrimp and other crustaceans provide food in a chain which in turn can harm bears and other large mammals.

The Guardian, Manchester: 31 March 1989

There were many anti-Gulf demonstrations abroad. In Australia, which has sent two frigates and one supply ship, thousands of protesters marched through cities shouting 'No blood for oil' . . . a handwritten sign taped to a New York City highway asked simply, 'Die For Gas?'

The Independent on Sunday, London: 20 January 1991

The peace movement to stop war in the Gulf showed its strength yesterday when tens of thousands of people turned out for demonstrations and marches across Europe . . . If there was a theme to the protests it was that . . . a conflict in the Gulf was not about justice, it was a war about oil.

The Independent on Sunday, London: 13 January 1991

While something akin to war fever has gripped the United States, some American soldiers have refused to go to the Middle East . . .

The most outspoken objector so far is Marine Corporal Jeffrey Paterson in Hawaii who said he would not fight for 'American profits and cheap oil' and is in a military prison for refusing to go to the Middle East.

The Guardian, Manchester: 7 September 1990

If in a certain place of the land naphtha [crude oil] oozes out, that country will walk in widowhood.

Cuneiform text from Babylonian tablet in the British Museum (CT. xxxix 10a^5), cited in R. J. Forbes, 'Petroleum and Bitumen in Antiquity', *Ambix, Journal for the Study of Alchemy and Early Chemistry*, Vol. II, 1938

At the town of Milovice, the site of the Soviet army's largest base and its headquarters in Czechoslovakia, Ales Kubes, leader of the local Civic Forum group, says: 'Pollution is everywhere. Oil and diesel fuel have poisoned underground water which feeds many of the wells. Nobody knows precisely what other chemicals have been dumped.

'There is more pollution than ever now; as the Soviet troops are leaving they are draining all their vehicles by letting the oil out on to the ground. It will take a 100 years before things return to normal.'

At a base near Silac, in Slovakia, there were 30 litres of kerosene surfacing on a patch of ground every day. 'There was so much of it we thought we had struck a new natural resource,' a local official said.

Askold Krushelnycky, 'Czech outrage at pollution by Soviet troops', *The European*, 25–27 May 1990

About 2,500 Californians can expect to die each year for the next decade as a result of cancers caused by exposure to toxic chemicals. The main industrial offenders – oil refining, petrochemicals . . . are the backbone of the state's economy. 'We are in danger of poisoning our own prosperity,' California's Lieutenant Governor Leo McCarthy said last month when releasing the report. 'For every dollar of new investment resulting from economic expansion, we are spending $2 managing toxic chemicals.'

New Scientist, London: 4 July 1985

The city of Cubatão, Brazil, which hosts twenty-four petrochemical and other industrial plants, has been dubbed the 'valley of death' by environmental groups. Barraged with extraordinary levels of particulates and other pollutants, the city's residents suffer high rates of respiratory disease, and a rising incidence of miscarriages, stillbirths, and birth defects was noted in 1980.

Erik P. Eckholm, *Down to Earth, Environment and Human Needs*, London: Pluto Press, 1980

Hundreds of young children live in the sewers that run under the Colombian capital, Bogotá . . . most of the children are using bazuco (a rough residue of cocaine) or they siphon petrol from cars and inhale the fumes.

Telegraph Magazine, London: 30 June 1990

The most bitter example of the market on the Amazonian peoples came during the rubber boom of 1894 to 1914, particularly in the Upper Amazon. In order to meet the increasing demand for rubber to provide tyres for . . . motor vehicles, indigenous peoples were forced into slavery or debt-bondage. The most notorious and well documented example was in the Putumayo region, now in Columbia, where the Casa Arana (a Peruvian concern which later became established as the British-based Peruvian Amazon Company) was condemned internationally for its maltreatment of the Indians [A. Gray, 'The Putumayo Atrocities Revisited', paper presented at Oxford University seminar on the State, Boundaries and Indians, 1990]. Considering the scale of the work, the environmental destruction wrought by the rubber boom was not as severe as the appalling effect on the indigenous peoples of the area, many of whom lost up to 90 per cent of their population through displacement, disease and murder.

Andrew Gray, 'Indigenous Peoples and the Marketing of the Rainforest', *The Ecologist*, Camelford (Cornwall): Vol. 20, No. 6, November/December 1990

The car consumes land at an alarming rate: 6.5 hectares per km is the motorway average in Britain. But adding in junctions and service stations, the figure is brought up to nearer 10 hectares. In central London, the car accounts for only 11 per cent of journeys to work, but it takes 85 per cent of the road space. A 3.7 m-wide road devoted to bikes has 5 times the people-carrying capacity as one twice as wide devoted to cars. One fifth of a modern city area is now devoted to the car.

But the car also takes land indirectly. Because of the 'L.A.' factor, in which modern people are assumed to be car-mobile, industry, schools, shops and hospitals are sited at greater distances from one another. The land-take per person in the West is therefore growing rapidly, in urban sprawl. The hearts of cities die as the car chokes them and renders them increasingly unattractive, whilst people flee to the suburbs and beyond in their commuter cars.

Richard North, *The Real Cost*, London: Chatto & Windus, 1986

There are more than 124 million cars and trucks on the road in the USA. Last year almost 8 million weren't reregistered . . . Imagine a billion tons of scrap. At this rate it'll hit 2 billion tons soon after year 2000. And to go with this mountain there'll be another equally tremendous hole in the ground.

Charles Fox, 'The death and resurrection of old blue', *Co-Evolution Quarterly*, California: No. 17, Spring 1978

You can't grow up on the west coast and ignore environmental issues. The west is so fragile, palpably fragile, there is so little water out here. Los Angeles is a perfect example, they are killing environments in the north, to get enough water to wash their cars with in the south!

Ursula le Guin, *Elle* magazine, London: March 1990

Cars harness only 10–20 per cent of the potential energy in their fuel. The rest is converted to pollutants and heat . . . but overall pollution continues to increase as more cars travel more miles.

New Internationalist, Oxford: No. 195, May 1989

For animals as large as ourselves, carbon monoxide is inescapably deadly. It kills by preventing the red blood cells from conveying oxygen to our tissues.

James Lovelock, *The Ages of Gaia, A biography of our living earth*, Oxford University Press, 1988

The first extermination centre was set up at Chelmo, Poland, in the fall of 1939. Three mobile gas vans, using the carbon monoxide from their exhausts, became the first instruments of mass murder. Primitive and in-efficient as this early extermination centre was, it reached a killing rate of 1000 a day. Soon the methods of mass destruction of Jews were refined and killing centres with permanent gas chambers, still using carbon monoxide, were opened.

Joseph Borkin, *The Crime and Punishment of I. G. Farben*, London: André Deutsch, 1979

Hitler himself is said to have decided upon the use of carbon monoxide as the killing method, on the so-called medical advice of Dr Heyde . . . The gas worked perfectly. The first Nazi gas chamber had been constructed under the supervision of Christian Wirth, of the SS Criminal Police . . . The arrangement included a fake shower room with benches, the gas being inserted from the outside into water pipes with small holes through which the carbon monoxide could escape. Present were two SS chemists with doctoral degrees, one of whom operated the gas. The other, August Becker, told how eighteen to twenty people were led naked into the 'shower room': through a peephole he observed that very quickly 'people toppled over, or lay on the benches' – all without 'scenes or commotion'.

Robert Jay Lifton, *The Nazi Doctors, A Study in the Psychology of Evil*, London: Macmillan, 1986

A wave of copycat suicides among apparently normal young people is causing serious concern to Italian parents and psychologists. In just over a week, 19 people have taken their lives for little apparent reason.

What is causing concern is that the method being used – carbon-monoxide poisoning in cars with the aid of a plastic tube – has become a macabre fad almost overnight. The suicides are arranged by pact among friends who choose one vehicle as if deciding to travel to a party. Most of the victims are working class, employed and from the industrial north.

Notes left behind are unemotional and decisive. Three youths from Alto Adige started the bizarre trend . . . Their note said simply: 'We are now rid of the trials of life.'

Bruce Johnston, 'Car suicide fad perplexes Italy', *Sunday Times*, London: 16 September 1990

Atmospheric levels of carbon monoxide must be taken as a significant contributory cause towards misjudgements prior to accidents.

Alan Wellburn, *Air Pollution and Acid Rain, The Biological Impact*, New York: John Wiley, 1988

People's senses become dulled by an hour's exposure to carbon monoxide levels of around 55 parts per million (a typical rush-hour level). A carbon monoxide level of 30 parts per million . . . has been found to impair the central nervous system in that part of the brain which controls perception and response.

J. H. Schulte, 'Effects of mild carbon monoxide intoxication', *Archives of Environmental Health*, November 1963

It wasn't until the arid 1950s that scientists led by Dr A. J. Haagen-Smit of the California Institute of Technology discovered that a major source of smog was automobile fumes . . . [that] every car in the nation on an average, emits more than 100 cubic feet of fumes every day.

Gladwin Hill, *The New York Times*, 28 September 1966

The Department of the Environment is about to give its pollution inspectors company cars at a time when the perk has never had a worse environmental image.

Company cars account for more than half of new car sales. The perk – which is encouraged by the income tax and national insurance systems – has also been responsible for driving up the body and engine size of the average car and increasing fuel consumption.

Environmentalists argued that it would encourage them to travel and pollute more, and to own more than one car.

The Independent, London: 13 June 1990

Airy-fairy environmentalists were attacked by Mrs Thatcher yesterday in a strong call for realism over pollution. The Prime Minister said: 'I find some people thinking of the environment in an airy-fairy way, as if we could go back to a village life. Some might quite like it, but it is quite impossible to do.'

There was no way we could do without 'the great car economy', she warned, because the economy would collapse if we did.

Kate Parkin, *Daily Express*, London: 17 March 1990

On the morning of Sept. 7, growers in the Westland region between Rotterdam and The Hague entered their hothouses to find most of their chrysanthemums shrivelled and dead, the victim of polluted air sucked into the greenhouses by ventilation systems. More than 100 growers in the Westland region lost part or all of their chrysanthemum crops that day, and their combined losses are estimated at up to 5 million guilders ($2.5 million). But even more worrying is the implication that air pollution in the Netherlands is sometimes so severe that it can suddenly kill off plants and crops.

So far, researchers have been able to establish only that the culprit was 'photochemical' air pollution – a situation caused when high concentrations of separate chemicals combine in the air to make deadly new compounds.

International Herald Tribune, Paris: 2 November 1989

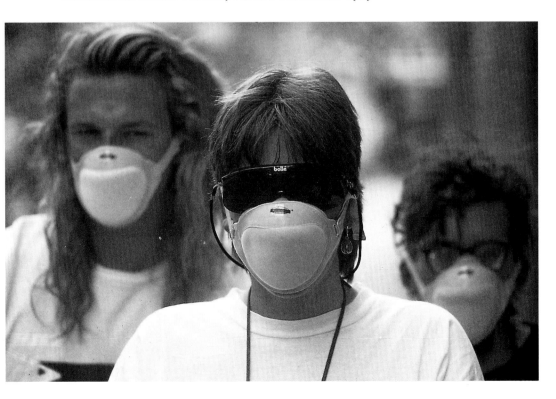

Every summer [in Athens] between six and ten people, mainly the elderly and the very young, are killed each day by the smog or *nefos*. Car pollution makes up about 85 per cent of this hot smog. Doctors in the city offer the parents of a baby a straight choice: fit your child with an oxygen mask or leave town.

Gareth Huw Davies, 'The road to ruin?' *Radio Times*, London: 2–8 December 1989

The most frequently given reason for living in Los Angeles is its many hours of sunshine. Yet it is this same solar benefit combining with the exhaust hydrocarbons from the eight million gallons of petrol burnt each day by four million vehicles that not only damages the eyes and destroys the lungs of those beneath the yellow blanket, but in fact blots out the very thing that brought them there in the first place.

Norman F. Dixon, *Our Own Worst Enemy*, London: Jonathan Cape, 1987

A child's IQ can be lowered by 5 per cent through growing up in a polluted inner city.

Sunday Times, London: 13 November 1988

In a study in Mexico City, 7 out of 10 newborns were found to have lead levels in their blood in excess of World Health Organisation norms. 'The implications to the Mexican society, that an entire generation of children will be intellectually stunted, is truly staggering,' says chemist and environmental activist Manuel Guerra.

Hilary F. French, *Clearing the Air: A Global Agenda*, Washington: Worldwatch Institute, January 1990

The choice of killing substance and the injection technique had a specific development in Auschwitz. There was considerable experimentation with other substances – benzine, gasoline, hydrogen peroxide, evipan and prussic acid (cyanide), and air – all injected into the veins.

Robert Jay Lifton, *The Nazi Doctors, A Study in the Psychology of Evil*, London: Macmillan, 1986

I regard Henry Ford as my inspiration.

Adolph Hitler, *Detroit News*, 31 December 1931

We look to Heinrich [Henry] Ford as the leader of the growing fascist party in America.

Adolph Hitler Interview, *Chicago Tribune*, 8 March 1923. Cited in Albert Lee, *Henry Ford and the Jews*, New York: Stein and Day, 1980

Significant levels of benzene, the cancer-causing agent in car exhaust emissions, have been found over Sheffield in the first monitoring exercise of its kind in Britain. Scientists fear that the levels could be even higher in other cities and towns, particularly London. Long-term effects could be very damaging.

A World Health Organisation report on air-quality guidelines says that 'no safe limit of benzene can be recommended as it is carcinogenic to humans and there is no safe threshold level.'

An alarming feature is that benzene levels are not reduced in unleaded petrol. Scientists say it can be found at even higher levels in super-unleaded, the so-called 'green power-fuel'.

Sunday Correspondent, London: 4 February 1990

Unleaded petrol still contains a small amount of lead.

Steve Elsworth, *A Dictionary of the Environment*, London: Paladin, 1990

There is now categorical proof that London's smog is twice as dangerous as that of Los Angeles. Cancer-causing benzene . . . has reached alarming levels. Dr Wolffe, a toxicologist at University College, London, blames benzene for many of the 'pockets' of leukaemia found around Britain in recent years . . . 'There is a link between leukaemia and towns with poor public transport and a heavy reliance on cars.' Dr Wolffe named Glenrothes, Corby, Peterlee and Aycliffe as good examples. Leukaemia levels were lower in dormitory or sleeper towns near London because of the good train and public transport systems. 'The truth is nobody really knows what a safe level for benzene is. But it is possible leukaemia has increased with the level of car ownership.'

Jim Gallagher, 'Our Smog Even More Lethal Than L.A.' *Today*, London: 24 August 1990

An American study has revealed that 12 per cent of lung cancer deaths in the USA could be attributed to motor vehicle emissions. No work in this area has been done in the UK, but if the figure is applicable to Britain, this would mean 3,000 to 4,000 lung cancer deaths per year as a result of automobile pollution.

Steve Elsworth, *A Dictionary of the Environment*, London: Paladin, 1990

Air pollution in Hungary has emerged as a major factor behind a dramatic decline in public health which has seen mortality rates slip back to the level of the 1930s, according to environmentalists. Their studies indicate that one death in 16 is now directly attributable to the growing menace, blamed largely on motor exhaust fumes.

It is alleged that the authorities are unwilling to see any reduction in petrol consumption as sales bring in £280 million a year in state revenues.

Daily Telegraph, London: 3 May 1989

Exhaust from diesel engines contains lower concentrations of some gaseous pollutants but higher concentrations of particulate bearing organic extracts including polyaromatic hydrocarbons. Evidence from experimental studies [Steenland K., 'Lung cancer and diesel exhaust; a review'. Am. J. Ind. Med. 1986: 10:177–89] shows that these are mutagenic and carcinogenic . . . With this in mind the British Lung Foundation recently recommended the use of masks for occupational groups exposed to high levels of particulates, particularly those who exercise – such as bicycle couriers.

Malcolm Green and Robert C. Read, *British Medical Journal*, 300, pp. 761–2, 24 March 1990

Dutch cars contribute more than 80 per cent of the country's air pollution from nitrogen oxides, a key component of both acid rain and photo-chemical smog.

New Scientist, London: 24-31 December 1988

The exhaust of an average car emits enough nitrogen oxides in a year to dissolve a 20 lb steel cannonball. As there are more than 20 million cars in Britain – and 400 million worldwide – that washes out into a flood of forest-killing acid rain.

Roger Bell, 'Cat-calls for a dirty British performance', *The Independent on Sunday*, London: 18 February 1990

Acid rain's most negative impacts have been on life in rivers and lakes. When the acidity of waters begins to rise, fish reproduction is impaired and calcium in fish skeletons becomes depleted, causing malformed 'hump-back' fish. Acidic waters also unlock aluminium from surrounding soils, which then builds up on fish gills. As water pH falls below 5.5, smaller species of crustaceans, plankton, molluscs, and flies begin to disappear. At a pH of 5.0 the decomposition of organic matter, the foundation of the aquatic food chain,

is undermined. Below a pH of 4.5 all fish are dead and the only remaining life is a mat of algae, moss, and fungus. Lacking organic matter, the water of an acidified lake assumes the crystal clarity of a swimming pool – a deceptive beauty indeed.

At least 5,000 of Sweden's lakes are seriously ill . . . All the lakes in a 13,000-square kilometre area of southern Norway are damaged . . .

In the Adirondack Mountains of upstate New York, officially declared 'forever wild' since 1892, more than half the lakes are in critical condition, more than 200 of them devoid of fish . . . Thousands more water bodies elsewhere in the United States, including lakes in the famed Boundary Waters area in northern Minnesota, have registered ominous rises in acidity . . .

Fish have disappeared completely from at least 140 Canadian lakes, mainly in Ontario, and life has been altered in thousands more. Scientists fear that as many as 48,000 of Canada's lakes could become fishless over the next decade.

Erik P. Eckholm, *Down to Earth, Environment and Human Needs*, London: Pluto Press, 1982

t Takes a Ford to Bring a Single One Home.

B MW has stopped shipping its cars through the port of Jacksonville, USA because acid rain is ruining the cars' paint. Other foreign auto companies are threatening to do the same.

BMW halted its shipments after a shower last summer left paint on 2000 cars pitted and scarred. This acid rain shower, the worst of eleven last year, dissolved the paint on some cars down to the metal.

Earth Island Journal, Earthwatch, Cork: No. 5, September–October 1987

Acid rain and air pollution is making trees in Britain some of the most badly damaged in Europe, only Czechoslovakia and Greece as badly affected among 21 European nations included in a survey published by the United Nations yesterday.

Broadleaf tree varieties are now showing signs of damage in Britain, with 64 per cent of woods and forests affected. Strong rises in defoliation were also reported by Sweden, Belgium, and Bulgaria.

The survey said oaks, especially those older than 60 years, showed a dramatic increase in defoliation last year, and in Britain, Holland and Czechoslovakia were especially critical.

The Guardian, Manchester: 8 July 1989

Carbon dioxide contributes far more to the greenhouse effect than previously thought . . . Research by Dr Dan Lashof, senior scientist at the National Resource Defence Council in Washington DC, shows that carbon dioxide contributes more than 80 per cent of the total warming.

Sunday Correspondent, London: 4 February 1990

Corrosion of historical monuments is particularly evident in Europe – from the Acropolis, to the Royal Palace in Amsterdam, to the medieval buildings and monuments of Krakow, Poland. Although some decay is to be expected in structures dating to antiquity, pollution is greatly speeding the process. T. N. Skoulikidis, a Greek specialist on acid corrosion, has estimated that Athenian monuments have deteriorated more in the past 20–25 years from pollution than in the previous 2,400 . . . In the Katowice region of southern Poland, trains must slow down in certain places because the railway tracks have corroded, apparently from acid rain.

Hilary F. French, *Clearing the Air: A Global Agenda*, Washington: Worldwatch Institute, January 1990

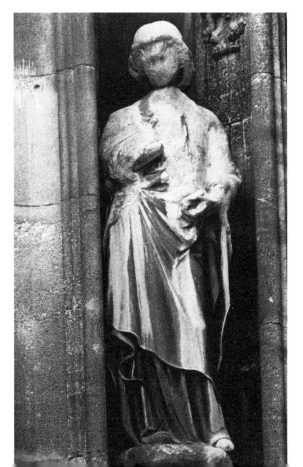

The air in Rome now has the highest concentration of carbon dioxide in the world. And this level, like the city itself, was not built up in one day, but over the last 35 years. During that period the number of locally-registered vehicles has risen from 30,000 to 1.5 million, or one for every two residents . . .

The Guardian, Manchester: 14 November 1986

Catalytic converters produce more carbon dioxide than normal, partly because the poisonous carbon monoxide is converted within the car instead of in the atmosphere, and with growing concern for the greenhouse effect, this makes the environmental equation more complicated.

Chris Baines, 'The Environmental Combustion Engine', *BBC Wildlife Magazine*, Bristol: October 1989

QUESTION: A catalytic converter in my car will convert poisonous carbon monoxide into carbon dioxide. Since carbon dioxide is thought to be the major cause of the greenhouse effect, am I really being 'green' if I use one?

The questioner is right that catalytic converters do nothing to prevent emissions of carbon dioxide . . . carbon dioxide accounts for about half of the enhanced greenhouse effects and, in the UK, road transport accounts for about one quarter of our emissions of CO_2. The only way of preventing your car emitting CO_2 is to stop using it.

Dr Keith Shine, Department of Meteorology, Reading University, *Notes and Queries*, *A Guardian Book*, compiled by Brian Whitaker, London: Fourth Estate, 1990

Catalytic converters kid people into believing their cars are eco-friendly. This is a false premise. For a start catalytic converters do not start to function until the engine reaches a working temperature of 300°C and will not perform optimally until 1000°C. As the majority of car journeys are of five miles or less (Source: Dept of Transport's National Travel Survey 1985–6) engines rarely get much past the first temperature. Using a car – no matter how catalytically converted – can never be Green. Get a bike instead.

Carlton Reid (Editor), *Whole Life*, Newcastle-upon-Tyne: From *Notes and Queries*, *A Guardian Book*, compiled by Brian Whitaker, London: Fourth Estate, 1990

The 'dustbowl' drought in America is '99 per cent certain to be an early manifestation of climatic changes, caused by pollution, which scientists have predicted for years, a leading space agency specialist has told a congressional committee.

Dr James Hansen said the evidence was that the 'greenhouse effect' – expected to cause a rise in world temperature and a series of droughts as infra-red rays from the sun are trapped in the atmosphere by carbon monoxide and other pollutants – had begun.

Statistics compiled by NASA show that the warming effect has gone beyond any previously logged variations. The expected results – drought, a drop in fresh water levels and an increase in the sea level as the ice-caps begin to melt – have already started.

Daily Telegraph, London: 25 June 1988

Then there are the real droughts, those that affect parts of the world where dry periods are measured in years rather than weeks . . . Does this [the greenhouse] effect explain the drought that afflicted Ethiopia some years ago, and the droughts in the Sahel region, along the southern edge of the Sahara? Again, some scientists think it may.

Michael Allaby, *Living in the Greenhouse, A Global Warning*, Wellingborough: Thorsons, 1990

February 1990. Sweden: Warmest February since records began in 1700 kept Stockholm harbour free from ice. Switzerland: One of the lowest snowfalls in 50 years. Britain: The warmest February since 1779. Highest winds for 30 years. Gales of up to 134 mph claimed 14 lives and left 2000 homeless in north Wales.

March 1990: Barely any snow in Oregon and Pennsylvania. Ski resorts remained closed. Britain: The warmest March for 22 years.

Weather Report No. 2, 'Storm Warning', *The Observer* Special, 15 April 1990

Worldwide, the six warmest years for which we have records were all in the 1980s. That doesn't *prove* the planet is heating up, any more than rolling 10 sevens in a row proves that the dice are loaded. But it does add urgency to this debate.

Bill McKibben, 'Planet earth and the point of no return', *The Independent*, London: 27 January 1990

The 'glass' in the world's greenhouse is a natural trap about 15–25 km above our heads at the top of the atmosphere, where some rising gases are normally contained, and which the sun's rays can penetrate. But gases are now being emitted at a faster rate . . . and this natural trap is thickening, causing more of the rising heat from the earth's surface to be reflected back. This causes global warming.

Chris Baines, 'Warming to the Problem', *Radio Times*, London: 3–9 June 1989

The type of society that would develop [in the greenhouse effect] is described by Dr Nicholas Middleton of Oxford University: 'In a heat-wave, the death rate would rise markedly. The lowest socio-economic groups confined to cities would suffer most' . . . The rising temperatures could lead to people becoming more irritable. There could be an increase in food poisoning. Bread, cakes and fresh produce would have a shorter shelf life. Insect swarms could invade Britain, and snakes become more abundant.

Sunday Times, London: 13 November 1988

For three years Brian Hoskins [Professor of Meteorology at Reading University], and Dr Paul Valdes, a research fellow in the same department, have been studying storms . . . According to a scenario they have drawn up, global warming may have increased the amount of water vapour in the atmosphere and this could have a direct effect on the severity of the storm.

Heating is required to turn sea water into water vapour, which rises into the atmosphere. As this water vapour condenses to form cloud or produce rain, heat is released back into the atmosphere. This 'stokes up' the storm and adds more energy into the swirling air systems as they head towards Britain. Hoskins calls it 'the scientific problem of the next decade . . . I believe what we are doing to our planet does have some effect. The dice may now be loaded against us.'

Sunday Times, London: 4 March 1990

The death toll from gale-force winds which ripped across France at the weekend rose to 23 yesterday after two people died of their injuries. Many victims were crushed to death as 90 mile an hour winds uprooted trees, tore roofs off houses and flung debris into the air. One woman in the Paris region, where 13 of the deaths occurred, was speared through the head by a metal shutter bar dislodged by a powerful gust. Dozens of people were injured, among them firemen, who answered 6000 emergency calls and worked throughout the night . . . Another six people were killed – five by falling trees – when the storms swept eastwards into West Germany.

Western Morning News, Plymouth: 5 February 1990

It would be a brave man who would say categorically that the storm [January, 1990] was not caused by the greenhouse effect.

Dr Geoff Jenkins (British representative on the Intergovernmental Conference on Climate Change), *The Observer*, London: 15 April 1990

The public was unaware of the enormous scale of the action that was needed to tackle the threat to the world's climate Sir Ian Lloyd (Havant, C), chairman of the select committee on energy, told MPs. Speaking in a Commons debate on world climate change and his committee's report on the greenhouse effect, he said that keeping man's tenancy on earth might require a worldwide programme by comparison with which all previous endeavours, even in war and in putting a man on the moon, 'will pale into insignificance'.

The Times, London: 10 November 1989

Proposals for carbon taxes to discourage people from burning fuels thus adding to the carbon dioxide emissions that cause global warming have been ruled out by the Secretary of State for the Environment . . . The Treasury argues that doubling the cost of motoring, which studies suggest would be needed to achieve a significant impact on carbon dioxide emissions, would send the retail price index through the roof.

The Independent on Sunday, London: 13 May 1990

The most ominous statistic to come out of the Australian conference [on global warming] yesterday, is the estimated sheer quantity of water now locked up in Antarctica in the form of ice.

It makes up 90 per cent of the water on the surface of the Earth, and if it all melted sea levels would rise by approximately 200 feet.

Daily Telegraph, London: 31 August 1988

David Everest, formerly chief scientific officer for environmental pollution at the Department of the Environment, says the worst effect of a 5°C rise in global temperature would be flooding. The sea could rise more than 1.5 metres. Indeed he believes that if ice breaks off in the Antarctic and falls into the sea it could cause 'surges', raising the water by as much as 5 metres. This would cover huge areas of Britain and force perhaps half the 56 m population to move inland.

Sunday Times, London: 13 November 1988

A dramatic thinning of the Arctic ice sheet over the past 10 years may be due to changing wind patterns and global warming caused by the greenhouse effect . . . Extensive surveys of the Arctic ice by Royal Navy submarines travelling under the icecap have shown that at least 15 per cent of the ice covering 115,000 square miles has melted since 1976.

The Independent on Sunday, London: 25 February 1990

Lecturer Keith Nichols and his wife Lorna have moved from their seafront flat at Exmouth to avoid the impact of the so-called greenhouse effect.

The Nicholses are so worried by the scientists' predictions that the warming of the atmosphere will lead to significant rise in sea levels they have gone to higher ground.

Their new bungalow home at Halsden Avenue is more than 50 feet above sea level which Mr Nichols says should make them safe from flooding. Mr Nichols, a psychology lecturer at Exeter University who before last month's move lived at Morton Crescent, said the estate agents who handled the sale thought they were 'nuts'.

Western Morning News, Plymouth: 3 May 1989

Low-level ozone is another greenhouse gas, formed in urban photochemical smogs in car-dominant cultures such as Los Angeles, Mexico and other large cities around the globe.

Chris Baines, 'Warming to the Problem', *Radio Times*, London: 3–9 June 1989

Why ozone is bad for you. Ozone, far from being the source of the bracing air of the seaside, is poisonous. Ordinarily, oxygen exists as a molecule containing two oxygen atoms. Ozone, however, contains three oxygen atoms: an ordinary oxygen molecule plus a highly reactive single oxygen atom.

Ozone is formed naturally in the upper atmosphere and has the valuable ability to block most of the Sun's ultraviolet rays and other harmful high-energy radiation, preventing it from reaching the Earth's surface.

If ozone is breathed in, however, in concentrated form, the spare oxygen atom is capable of reacting with living tissue, damaging it in much the same way as ordinary oxygen damages iron by turning it to rust. The effect of the damage is to alter the tissues of the lungs so that oxygen can no longer reach the blood-stream. As a result, the victim dies, paradoxically from a lack of oxygen.

The bracing smell of the seaside? That is usually derived from rotting seaweed.

Reader's Digest Book of Facts, London: Hodder & Stoughton, 1985

Ozone is now coming down to earth in the form of photochemical smog. This is mainly the fault of the internal combustion engine.

New Scientist, London: 19 September 1985

For several days during most summers, Europe is bathed in ozone at concentrations that would be illegal if created in a factory. Unlike the protective shield of ozone high in the stratosphere, this ozone at ground level is largely man-made, and it is dangerous. It is created by sunlight acting on a range of pollutants, especially from car exhausts. The ozone causes attacks of asthma in humans, eats at every kind of material from rubber bands and car tyres to textiles, stunts the growth of plants and may be an important cause of the decline of Europe's trees.

Fred Pearce and Steve Elsworth, 'Stalled in a haze of ozone', *New Scientist*, London: 20 November 1986

Outside the picturesque Butcher's Arms pub in Oakridge, ozone levels built up to danger point by 7 pm on Friday. At 100 parts per billion, it was the level at which the World Health Organisation warns that the health of ordinary people is being endangered. And yesterday, tests in Stroud showed the level rose above 100 ppb.

In the short term, it can lead to dizziness, headaches, eye irritation, shortness of breath, and nausea. In the long term, doctors believe it could break down the body's immune system and create respiratory illness.

Mail on Sunday, London: 22 July 1990

Despite oil industry claims that further regulation of ozone is not cost-effective, it has been estimated in the US that the health of 28 million children is at risk from ozone, that childhood asthma has increased 25 per cent from 1982 to 1986, that over 750,000 children were hospitalised with respiratory disease in 1987, and that deaths from chronic lung disease have increased 36 per cent since 1970.

Samuel S. Epstein, 'The Real Cost of Petrol', *The Ecologist*, Camelford (Cornwall): vol. 19, No. 4, July/August 1989

S mog may punch holes in condoms, researchers have reported. The culprit is ozone, said a report from California University.

The Independent, London: 9 September 1988

O zone molecules are constantly being made. But they can be destroyed by any of a number of chemical processes. For example, the stratosphere receives regular injections of nitrogen-bearing compounds such as nitrous oxide. Produced by fossil-fuel combustion . . . the gas rides the rising air currents to the top of the troposphere. Forced higher still by the tremendous upward push of tropical storms, it finally enters and percolates slowly into the stratosphere.

'The Heat Is On', *Time Magazine*, New York: 19 October 1987

S cientists believe they have found the first evidence that man-made chemicals have opened up a hole in the Earth's protective ozone layer over the Arctic . . . until now scientists were not able to prove that the same destruction was taking place above the North Pole, although a group of 200 Western experts who visited the area in January and February predicted that it could happen this year.

The hole, identified after a massive column of the ozone-damaging chemicals moved into sunlight over northern Scandinavia last month, poses a long-term threat to life in large parts of the northern hemisphere. It means that some of the most populated parts of the globe, including northern Europe, North America, and the Soviet Union, will have less protection from the damaging rays of the sun if the hole – more accurately a thinning – appears every year. The effects could include an increase in cancers and eye cataracts, damage to marine life, reduced crop yields and rising global temperatures.

Sunday Times, London: 5 March 1989

T he ozone hole over the Antarctic is now at least as large as it was in 1987 – the deepest recorded. This year's measurements have convinced scientists that massive ozone depletion above the Antarctic in the spring is likely to continue for 50 years or more.

The Guardian, Manchester: 13 October 1989

T heir cosmology [the Yanomami of the Amazon] is a rich and complete explanation of their place in the forest; a kaleidoscope of experience, knowledge and magic. They foretell the end of the world when the Yanomami end. The *nabe* [foreigners] will die with the last Yanomami.

Davi Yanomami [spokesperson for the Yanomami] says that the mania of the whites to make smoke from motors . . . is spreading epidemics throughout the world. The sky is becoming poisoned with this smoke and the whole world is becoming ill.

The magic of other *shabonos* [villages] was blamed when the epidemics first killed Yanomami. But as the miners and their machines came nearer, the evil was said to come from the exhaust smoke . . . The death of shamans from this smoke, weakens the survivors' ability to keep order in the universe, to maintain the sky on its feet. 'Each time a shaman dies, the spirits within him are furious, they are liberated and they are extremely angry and begin to cut the feet of the sky. Only the other shamans can contain this spirit and keep the sky on its feet. So if all the Yanomami shamans die, then soon the sky will end by falling on the heads of everyone and not only the Yanomami but the whole of humanity will die.'

Dennison Berwick, 'At Death's Door', *Sunday Times Magazine*, London: 9 September 1990

On that 1st of October, 1924, I was assisting in the titanic rebirth of a new phenomenon . . . traffic.

Cars, cars, fast, fast! One is seized, filled with enthusiasm, with joy . . . the joy of power. The simple and naive pleasure of being in the midst of power, of strength. One participates in it. One takes part in this society that is just dawning. One has confidence in this new society: it will find a magnificent expression of its power. One believes in it.

Le Corbusier, *The City of Tomorrow*, translated by Frederick Etchells (1929), reprinted by The Architectural Press, London, 1971

The US Department of Transport estimates that nearly three billion gallons of gasoline were burned up in 1984 as American motorists stewed in traffic jams.

Michael Renner, *Rethinking the Role of the Automobile*, Washington: Worldwatch Institute, June 1988

The machines will turn to run into one another, traffic will tangle up in a long-drawn-out crash of collision

D. H. Lawrence, 'The Triumph of the Machine', *The Collected Poems of D. H. Lawrence*, vol. II, London: Heinemann, 1964

Contemporary nightmare: people are all getting into their cars and taking to the streets. They think they're going to get away somewhere safe. They think that, even though they have been told it's pointless. My parents push me and my sister into our car. They don't think about food or clothes or nothing. Then as soon as we get to the main road it's blocked with cars. People are honking their horns and screaming and wailing. And I think, this is how it's going to end – we're all going to die in a great big traffic jam.

Graham Swift, *Waterland*, London: Heinemann, 1983

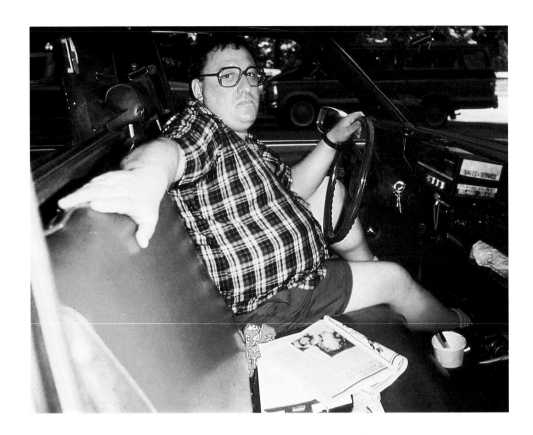

People who now agree that traffic congestion is throttling many cities still drive through them.

Alisdair Aird, *The Automotive Nightmare*, London: Hutchinson, 1972

Motor trucks [in New York] average less than six miles per hour in traffic, as against eleven miles per hour for horse drawn vehicles in 1911.

The New York Times, 13 March 1961

Britain is becoming a nation of car junkies, utterly dependent on the four-wheeled monster and apparently willing to put up with more crowded roads, traffic wardens, and even wheel clamps, despite a remarkably strong concern for the effects of motoring on the environment.

Within two years, half Britain's drivers will come from two-, three- or four-car families, an increase of a quarter on present levels of multiple ownership. An extra 2.5 m cars will then roll on to the already overcrowded highways. Households with five, six and seven cars are already a statistical reality.

Sunday Times, London: 12 February 1989

Motorists were branded 'heartless' after they pushed aside two crashed cars with injured pensioners trapped inside, in their rush to get to work in Basingstoke.

Western Morning News, Plymouth: 30 November 1990

The roads White Paper *Roads for Prosperity*, published on 18 May 1989, predicts an increase in traffic of 142 per cent by the year 2025 if the economy grows at a rate of 3 per cent per year until that time . . . an increase of 27.5 million vehicles. What would another 27.5 million vehicles look like?

Traffic jams these days are commonly measured in miles. Allowing 20 feet for each car (the recommended allowance for in-line parking), and assuming, conservatively, that the average size of the other vehicles (vans, lorries, buses and coaches, and motorcycles) is no larger than the average car, then another 27.5 million vehicles would form a queue 104,000 miles long. This could be accommodated, if stationary, on a new motorway stretching from London to Edinburgh – if it were 257 lanes wide.

John G. U. Adams (Department of Geography, University of London), 'Car ownership forecasting: Pull the ladder up, or climb back down?' *Traffic Engineering and Control*, March 1990

Los Angeles has 3.3 million motorised commuters morning and evening, and 77 per cent of the cars have only one person in them.

Richard North, *The Real Cost*, London: Chatto & Windus, 1986

Fear of driving on the M25 proved too much for a lorry driver who, unable to cope with the nose-to-tail traffic, hanged himself in a fit of despair, an inquest at Hitchin, Herts, was told yesterday.

Daily Telegraph, London: 27 November 1989

A cyclist comfortably beat all other transport through London's rush hour yesterday morning, taking less than half the time of a taxi and a third the time of a pedestrian. Contestants left Islington at 8.45, and Dave Godden, the cyclist, arrived 11 minutes later. The car driver took 17 minutes; the taxi, 23; the tube passenger, 28; and the pedestrian, 37. The car driver's time was possible only because he drove straight into Guildhall instead of looking for a parking place first.

The Guardian, Manchester: 5 June 1990

Obviously one desirable means of transportation would be something efficient, non-polluting, simple to manufacture and repair, energy-conserving, cheap, and harmless. It just so happens that such a means is available, indeed widely available, and has been so for nearly a century: the bicycle. S. S. Wilson of the Department of Engineering Science puts the case neatly:

> The contrast between the bicycle and the motor car is a very good illustration of technology on a human scale. The bicycle is a supreme example of ergonomics – the optimum adaptation of a machine to the human body, so that it uses this power efficiently. Hence the worldwide success of the bicycle and its derivations in meeting the real needs of the people in both rich and poor countries, with a minimum demand for energy and raw materials or ill effect on the environment. The motor car, on the other hand,

is a machine of inhuman scale as regards its size, its weight, its power (from 100 to 1000 times that of the driver himself) or its speed.

In terms of translating energy into transportation, there is *nothing*, neither animal nor mechanical, that is superior to a human being on a bicycle . . .

Kirkpatrick Sale, *Human Scale*, London: Secker & Warburg, 1980

Biking may be wonderful exercise and environmentally sound, but few individuals will be willing to pedal down roads where cars and trucks zoom past them with inches to spare, leaving the biker to wobble in a blast of air. Until roads are built with bike lanes or at least wide shoulders, few people are likely to get in the habit of biking. Even with those improvements, it will take a shifting of attitudes to get most people to take up two-wheel travel. People will need to believe that even one less trip in the car adds up to something, that riding a bicycle is, like recycling paper or conserving electricity, an endeavour worth pursuing. Deciding to ride a bike is taking on responsibility: Not everyone will choose to do so, but for everyone who does, the world, rest assured, will be at least a little better off.

Jane Bosveld, 'Can Bicycles Save the World?', *Omni*, New York: February 1989

When I see an adult on a bicycle, I have hope for the human race.

H. G. Wells, 1866–1946

The United States puts 45 per cent of its total energy into vehicles: to make them, run them and clear a right of way for them. For the sole purpose of transporting people, 250 million American citizens allocate more fuel than is used by 1,300 million Chinese and Indians for all purposes. Almost all this fuel is burnt in a rain dance of time-consuming acceleration . . . The typical American male devotes more than 1,600 hours a year to his car. He sits in it while it goes and while it stands idling. He parks it and searches for it. He earns the money to put down on it and to meet the monthly instalments. He works to pay for petrol, tolls, insurance, taxes, and tickets. He spends four of his sixteen waking hours on the road or gathering his resources for it. And this figure does not take into account the time consumed by other activities dictated by transport: time spent in hospitals, traffic courts and garages . . . The model American puts in 1000 hours to get 9000 miles; less than five miles an hour.

In countries deprived of a transportation industry, people manage to do the same, walking wherever they want to go, and they allocate only three to eight per cent of their society's time budget to traffic instead of 28 per cent.

Ivan D. Illich, *Energy and Equity*, London: Calder & Boyars, 1974

Annihilate time and space as you may, a man's stride remains the true standard of distance; an eternal and unalterable scale.

Kenneth Grahame, *Pagan Papers*, London: Elkin Matthews & John Lane, 1898

Some of the Greek philosophers rightly associated thought with walking, and were for that reason called peripatetic. But walking in our time, like philosophy in our time, has declined to a state of paralysis. The paths across the fields have long since been ploughed away; even bridle-paths which in my childhood were busy with human traffic have completely disappeared. The cause of this rapid obliteration of pathways: the internal combustion engine . . . The price that has been paid is the end of a way of life out of which whatever poetry and intelligence we possess arose as naturally as poppies and cornflowers from the undisciplined earth, and the alienation of sensibility that is the inevitable consequence of mechanization. We have lost the physical experience that comes from a direct contact with the organic processes of nature . . . elementally human experiences that to be deprived of them is to become something less than human. There has never been and never can be a civilization that is not rooted in such organic processes. We know it – instinctively we know it – and go like blind animals into a darker age than history has ever known.

Herbert Read, *The Contrary Experience*, London: Faber & Faber, 1963

'I am certain,' said Mr Escot, 'that a wild man can travel an immense distance without fatigue; but to what is the advantage of locomotion? The wild man is happy in one spot, and there he remains: the civilised man is wretched in every place he happens to be in, and then congratulates himself on being accommodated with a machine, that will whirl him to another, where he will be just as miserable as ever.'

Thomas Love Peacock, *Headlong Hall*, London: Bentley, 1816

Only a few years ago your average sociologist, asked to envision the city of the future, pointed without hesitation to Los Angeles.
That was the lifestyle we were all headed for . . . That was the Tomorrow's City visible today, the city of multilane freeways, the city of the automobile, to which its inhabitants adhere as tenaciously as a hermit crab to its shell, where there are districts where a human biped denuded of any conveyance and primitively ambulating along a pavement is so disconcerting a sight as to call for instant interrogation by the police.

Elaine Morgan, *Falling Apart, The Rise and Decline of Urban Civilisation*, London: Souvenir Press, 1976

God set a limit to man's locomotive ambition in the construction of his body. Man immediately proceeded to discover means of over-riding the limit.

Mahatma Gandhi, 1869–1948

A race that neglects or despises this primitive gift, that fears the touch of the soil, that has no footpaths, no community of ownership in the land

which they enjoy, that warns off the walker as a trespasser, that knows no way but the highway, the carriage-way, that forgets the stile, the footbridge . . . is in a fair way to far more serious degeneracy.

John Burroughs, 'The Exhilarations of the Road in Winter Sunshine' from *In Praise of Walking*, Boston: Houghton, Osgood, 1875

When a motor vehicle is travelling so fast that it cannot pull up quickly enough to avoid knocking down a pedestrian, the horn is blown. This is called a warning.

J. B. Morton, *Morton's Folly*, London: Sheed and Ward, 1933

The number of pedestrians and cyclists killed on the road has increased since car drivers have been compelled to wear seat belts.

Last week, the Department of Transport published details of road deaths for a 20-month period from February 1983, when seat belts were made compulsory for people in the front seats of cars, to September 1984. They show that the number of car drivers killed fell by 421, compared with the corresponding period in 1981 and 1982. The number of front-seat passengers who were killed also fell, by 235. However, the number of pedestrians killed by cars in the same period rose by 77 and the number of pedal cyclists killed rose by 63. This unwanted effect of the seat-belt laws was predicted in 1981 by a paper prepared at the Department of Transport (DoT). The paper was suppressed because of its uncomfortable conclusions, and became public earlier this year only after details were published in *New Scientist* (7 February, p. 7).

This increase in pedestrian deaths was first forecast by John Adams, a geography lecturer at University College, London. He argued that forcing drivers to wear belts would make them feel safer. As a result they would drive more dangerously, in much the same way as a trapeze artist might perform more daring tricks with a safety net than without one. The result would be an increase in the number of pedestrians and pedal cyclists being hit by cars. Adams' forecast was supported by the DoT's paper which described the likelihood of an increase in pedestrian deaths as 'alarming'.

Mick Hamer, 'Belted drivers are killing more pedestrians', *New Scientist*, London: 25 April 1985

The case against cars does not depend on moralistic remarks about children crushed to death on the way home from school. There is a respectably hedonistic case: the pleasure to be derived from cars is so mediocre compared to the delight of doing away with them.

Andrew Gimson, 'Motorised responsibility', *Spectator*, London: 23 February 1985

Vandals poured thousands of gallons of water into a petrol storage tank at the Dunmore service station in Shaldon, Devon, yesterday, and 20 motorists who filled up broke down after driving 300 yards.

Daily Telegraph, London: 18 June 1990

Jay Calascione was on her way back from a family party, reflecting on a rare moment of celebration. Her mood changed when she was a few yards from home in the village of Crowhurst, East Sussex and saw a Mini, adorned with rows of spotlights, glinting against the fading sunlight. In her words, the 52-year-old teacher 'snapped'.

She ran inside to find an axe. She returned and smashed up the Mini, which belonged to the man responsible for a road accident at the same spot 18 months earlier in which her 20-year-old son, Simon, died. He had been thrown from his Honda motorcycle. Mrs Calascione says, without remorse, that smashing the car 'was the best thing I ever did'.

The Independent, London: 29 August 1990

The bootblack . . . knew the gossip, he watched the street constantly, he changed up notes at the cafe and he swept up the cafe floor when he had no customers. He usually had rumours to impart. That morning there was a car pyromaniac at work in the city. In the bad days there had been few cars in Barcelona. The 19th-century quarter, the Ensanche, was not designed for traffic. For many years after the Civil War its boulevards and plazas were empty of traffic. Today they are choked. Someone did not like this: the man now running loose in the city had a grudge against cars. A few years ago a pyromaniac had accounted for about 200 vehicles. He was in prison but he had a successor. One had to be careful. Guarded car parks were no use. The pyromaniac frequently struck here. Hmmm.

Patrick Marnham, 'A Place Apart', *The Independent Magazine*, London: 8 December 1990

Things got too much for author Kudno Mojesic. He was arrested in the street outside his Belgrade [Yugoslavia] home attacking cars with an axe, yelling 'Away with all cars – they are the devil's work.'

Sunday Mirror, London: 11 January 1976

S tone-throwing attacks on motorists in a few lower-class New York City neighbourhoods became serious enough to require special police protection along several thoroughfares. These attacks were attributed to the disruption of street games by motor vehicles because at this season of the year the city's streets become the playgrounds for children and the interruption of their sports by passing vehicles, especially automobiles, is often resented in as forcible an expression as they are capable of.

'To prevent Ruffian attacks on Automobiles in NY City', 13: 585 (June 1, 1904) in *Haselen Age*, cited in James T. Flink, *America Adopts the Automobile, 1890–1914*, Cambridge, Mass: MIT Press, 1975

In early 1969, Mayor John Lindsay of New York came to see me. I have always liked the imagination of this man. Lindsay and I have the same concern for what the automobile is doing to the quality of American life; in fact, the Mayor once remarked, while riding in a helicopter over New York, 'If I had a laser gun, I'd destroy all those cars down there.'

Walter J. Hickel, *Who Owns America*, New York: Prentice-Hall, 1972

S TOP THE CARS. I bought 5000 roofing nails from Bowery Lumber, great bags of fat 2-inch flat-topped roofing nails. We threw them on the streets and under the tyres of passing automobiles.

STOP THE CARS. STOP AIR POLLUTION.

THE AIR BELONGS TO THE PEOPLE AND NO ONE HAS THE RIGHT TO TURN IT TO POISON.

In the early evening, my crew and I seeded the streets with flat-topped roofing nails. First we stashed the bags of nails in safe storage under entrance steps, inside garbage cans, in doorways, and in waste baskets on street corners where we could just reach in and grab handfuls. I threw them like chickenfeed on the cobblestones of Greene Street. I would wait for the traffic to pass, and throw fistfuls of nails at 50-foot intervals . . .

For hours we moved through SOHO, coming out of parallel blocks and rendezvousing on Canal Street. Those were some of the great moments. Not during red lights, but when they turned green and the heavy fast-moving Sunday night Memorial Day weekend traffic to New Jersey sped along Canal

Street to the Holland Tunnel, we threw fistfuls of nails under their tyres. It was exhilarating and perfectly accomplished.

We got reports that traffic was blocked in the Holland Tunnel. Cars with flats in the Tunnel, on the other side, and going into it. So we moved away from that area. The streets of SOHO were polka-dotted with cars with flat tyres. We hit about 500 cars. The crowning achievement of the night was we got 3 cop cars, two on Greene, and one on Mercer. I walked up to one of the wrecked police cars (two flat tyres), and asked, 'Officer, what's happening?'

He looked at me and said, 'Some nut is nailing the street.'

John Giorno, ABSOLUTE MALICE AND JOY, from *Pranks, Devious Deeds and Mischievous Mirth*, San Francisco: Re/Search Publications, 1987

A great many things are going to change. We shall learn to be masters rather than servants of Nature.

Henry Ford (with Samuel Crowther), *My Life and Work*, London: Heinemann, 1922

It is upon one's feet, walking in a lonely footway, and not upon a tarred road in an automobile that one reaches God.

T. F. Powys, *Bottle Path and Other Stories*, London: Chatto & Windus, 1946

Now the Mama [holy man] grows sad,
He feels weak.
He says that the Earth is decaying.
The Earth is losing its strength
because they [the 'Younger Brothers', people of the Western world]
have taken away much petrol,
coal,
many minerals . . .

We tell you,
we the people of this place,
Kogi,
Asario,
Arhuaco:
that is a violation . . .
The Earth feels.
They take out petrol,
it feels pain there.
So the Earth sends out sickness.
There will be many medicines,
drugs,
but in the end the drugs will not be of any use . . .

Divination by a Mama of the Kogi tribe, Colombia – from Alan Ereira, *The Elder Brothers*, London: Jonathan Cape, 1990

G ive up haste and activity. Close your mouth. Only then will you compre-
hend the spirit of Tâo.

Lao-Tzu

Picture Credits

The publishers and I would like to thank the following for their kind permission to reproduce illustrations: Rene Burri/Magnum (p.1); Della Rosa (p.2); © C. Cross/ Uniphoto (p.8 centre); Harry Redl/Black Star/Colorific! (p.8 bottom); Jodi Cobb/National Geographic (p.9); Guy Nicholls (p.10 top); Piers Cavendish/Impact Photos (p.10 bottom); John Hill (p.11 top); D. Reed/Magnum (p.11 bottom); John Hill (p.14); John Hill (p.15 top); John Hill (p.15 centre); Ethan Hoffman (p.15 bottom); Ovak Arslanian/Imagine/ Impact Photos (p.16 top); Michael K. Nichols/Magnum (p.16 bottom); John Hill (p.17 top); Ethan Hoffman (p.17 bottom); John Hill (p.18 top); John Hill (p.18 bottom); John Hill (p.19 top); © G. Fritz/Uniphoto (p.20 bottom); John Hill (p.20 top); Michael K. Nichols/Magnum (p.21); © David Ryan/Uniphoto (p.22 top); Alex Bartel/Science Photo Library (p.22 bottom); John Hill (p.23 top); John Daniels/Ardea (p.23 bottom); © Bob Daenwich/Uniphoto (p.24); A. Hart-Davis/Science Photo Library (p.25); Martin Dohrn/ Science Photo Library (p.26); Burt Glinn/Magnum (p.27 top); John Hill (p.27 bottom); Tony Stone Worldwide (p.28 bottom); Barry Lewis/Network (p.29); Ullstein Bilderdienst (p.30 left and right); John Hill (p.31); Anna Tully/Hutchison Library (p.31 bottom); Barry Lewis/Network (p.32 bottom); Tony Stone Worldwide (p.33 top); Barry Lewis/ Network (p.34 top); Barry Lewis/Network (p.34 bottom); Barry Lewis/Network (p.35); Merideth Grierson (p.36); John Hill (p.38 top); John Hill (p.39 top left); John Hill (p.39 top right); Barry Lewis/Network (p.39 bottom); Zefa (p.40); © J. Olive/Uniphoto (p.41 top); Heathcote Williams (p.41 bottom); Zefa (p.42); Zefa (p.44); Phil Jude/Science Photo Library (p.45); Zefa (p.46 top); Nick Gordon/Ardea (p.46 bottom); A. & H. Frieder Michler/Science Photo Library (p.47 top); Zefa (p.47 bottom); Elizabeth Bomford/Ardea (p.48 bottom); Tony Stone Worldwide (p.48 top); © L. Ruggeri/Uniphoto (p.49 top); Rapho M. Frandream/Science Photo Library (p.49 bottom); © Frank Siteman/Uniphoto (p.50 top); © G. Morton/Uniphoto (p.50 bottom); Rene Burri/Magnum (p.51 top); © S. van Steyn/Uniphoto (p.51 bottom); Mike McQueen/Impact Photos (p.52 top); Zefa (p.52 bottom); Tomas Sennett/Contact/Colorific! (p.53 top); Enrico Ferorelli/Colorific! (p.53 bottom); J. R. Eyerman/Life Magazine © Time Warner Inc. December 22 1958/Katz (p.54/55); Barry Lewis/Network (p.56 top); Tomas Sennett/Contact/Colorific! (p.56 bottom); Ullstein Bilderdienst (p.57); S. Retick/Colorific! (p.58); Frank Spooner Pictures (p.59 top); Townsend Dickinson/Science Photo Library (p.59 bottom); Stuart Franklin/ Magnum (p.60); Paul Fusco/Magnum (p.61); P. Goycolea/Hutchison Library (p.63 top); G. Giansanti/Sygma (p.64); John Sturrock/Network (p.63 bottom); Ernst Haas/John Hillelson Agency (p.65 top); John Hill (p.65 bottom); John Hill (p.66); © T. Stephen Thompson/Uniphoto (p.67); Mike Wells (p.68); Paul Huf/Art Unlimited (p.69 top); Michael Gilbert/Science Photo Library (p.69 bottom); Zefa (p.70 top); NASA/Science Photo Library (p.70 bottom); NASA/Science Photo Library (p.71); Zefa (p.73); Bill Coleman (p.74); John Hill (p.75 top left); Tony Stone Worldwide (p.75 top right); John Hill (p.75 centre left); John Hill (p.75 centre right); John Hill (p.75 bottom left); John Hill (p.75 bottom right); John Hill (p.76); Barry Lewis/Network (p.77); John Hill (p.78 top); John Arthur/Impact Photos (p.78 bottom); Susan Meiselas/Magnum (p.79 top left); Gerd Ludwig/Katz (p.79 top right); Rene Burri/Magnum (p.79 bottom); Rene Burri/Magnum (p.80 top); Barry Lewis/Network (p.80 centre); John Hill (p.80 bottom); G. Bernard/ NHPA (p.83); Hulton Picture Company (p.84); Raissa Page (p.85); Barbara Norfleet (p.86); Hulton Picture Company (p.89); John Hill (p.89 bottom); British Film Institute (p.91 top); Eli Reed/Magnum (p.91 bottom); John Hill (p.93); Zefa (p.94); John Hill (p.95); Thomas Kelsey (p.97); Ullstein Bilderdienst (p.98); John Hill (p.99); ROSPA (p.102); Camera Press (p.104 top); Jill Freedman (p.104 bottom); Roger Mayne (p.106); Sygma (p.107); Guy Nicholls (p.108); Robert V. Eckert/Colorific! (p.109); Topham Picture Library (p.111); Spence Air Photos/L.A. Times (p.112); Eric Meacher/Katz (p.113); Pedro Meyer (p.115); Alen MacWeeny (p.116); Barry Lewis/Network (p.117); Richard Baker/Katz (p.119); Bossu/Sygma (p.122); Rene Burri/Magnum (p.123); Peter Addis (p.124); Richard Baker/Katz (p.127); Mike Goldwater/Network (p.128); James Stevenson/Science Photo Library (p.129); Richard House/Hutchison Library (p.132); Rene Burri/Magnum (p.133); Rick Maiman/Sygma (p.134); Zefa (p.136); Barry Lewis/Network (p.137); Bill Colman (p.139); Zefa (p.140); Topham Picture Library (p.141); John Hill (p.142 top); Friends of the Earth (p.142 bottom); Susan Jannsen (p.143); Stephen Dalton/NHPA (p.144); Felicity Nock (p.145); Nancy Durrell McKenna/Hutchison Library (p.146).

Acknowledgments

Grateful acknowledgments to Richard Adams of AdCo; Tony Allen; Don Atyeo; Joan Ball; Sal Shuel of BAPLA; Simon Barrett; Bob Bassara; Martin Beck; Guy Bentinck; Violanda Bersey; Margaret Bickerstaff; Daniel Brand; Anne Brewer; Steve Bricknell; George Bruce; Leah Bruce; Simon Burry; Jerome Byrne; Elke Cann; Jenny Cottom, Tim Chester, Mon Mohan, Rachael Kerr, Hilary Turner, Sarah Wherry and Sarah Wiesendanger of Jonathan Cape; Pascal Cariss, Tony Colwell, Roy Hutchins, Jonangus Mackay, Polly Samson, Diana Senior, Paul Sieveking, Elizabeth Smith and Joebear Webb for invaluable textual suggestions; Dave Cawse; Pete Chesterfield; Janice Clook; Mark Cohen; Mark Collingwood; Celia Cooper; Jeremy and Judith Curry; Anthea Morton-Saner, Julia Kreitman and Anna Sheppard of Curtis Brown; Curly Davis; Peter Dover; Kate Duffy for assiduous picture research; Joanne Eastment; Jago Eliot; Dee and Jules Evans; Lesley Fairbairn; Bob Flag; Adrian Flood; Lita Floyd; Sarah Foot; Alan Ford; Steven Fuller; Jill Furmanovsky; Fay Godwin; Patrick Gribbin; Keith Hack; Robin Hanbury-Tenison; Max Handley; John Hay; Jane Hill; John Hill; Clive Hooper; Takae Horton; Adrian Howe; Ian Irvine; Neal D. Jackson; Jay Jeffrey Jones; Peter Jukes; Paul Krassner; John Lahr; Mike Laity; Andrew Lanyon; Jo Lanyon; Lil Lanyon; Chris Lawrence; Dave Lawton; Warren Leming; Robert Lenkiewicz; Mike Lesser; Bill Levy; Chris Bray and Gilly Hancox of Logo; William MacAdams; Christine McArthur; Annette and George MacCallum; Marilyn McDougal; John May; Roger Mayne; John Michael; George Morley; Leon Morris; Virginia Kennedy of *Nature*; Kevin O'Reilly; Kevin Hill of Optikos Laboratories; Ted Orchard; Pete Orgill; Deborah, Ernest and Jean Parkins; Dave Patton; Fred Pearce; John Pearson; Sue Davies of the Photographers Gallery; Werner Pieper; Eddi Piper; Liz Orange and Michael Sewell of the Polytechnic Bookshop; Rex Pyke; Benedict Read; Russ Ainsworth of RMA Recording; Paul Robinson; P. St Germans; Lance Samson; Clio Smeeton; Hilary Stevens; Terry Stewart; Mike Sullivan; Charlotte Sankey of Survival International; Kim Taplin; Dave and Jane Taylor; Geoff Toms; Phyllis Treitel; Nerissa Trenear-Harvey; Christine Cross of TSW; Alan Underwood; Kathy Waite; Tracy Ward; John Warner; Jasper Watson; Lyall Watson; Angela Wells; Shaun Whiteside; Nicki and Tom Wildy; Martin Wilkinson; China Williams; Lily Williams; Liz Williams; Joe Winnington; Esther and William Worthy; Richard Worthy for meticulous co-ordination; Bill and Cory Wroath; Francis Wyndham; Heidrun Böhm and Lutz Kroth of Zweitausendeins.

Index

First published 1991
© Heathcote Williams 1991
Jonathan Cape, 20 Vauxhall Bridge Road, London SW1V 2SA

Heathcote Williams has asserted his right
under the Copyright, Designs and Patents Act 1988
to be identified as the author of this work

A CIP catalogue record for this book
is available from the British Library

ISBN 0-224-02644-5 (paperback)
0-224-02645-3 (hardback)

Printed in Italy by New Interlitho SpA, Milan